We Speak the Word of the Lord

A Practical Plan for More Effective Preaching

Daniel E. Harris

Paul – It was good to spend quality time in NJ – May God Bless you ministry of preaching always

Dan

ACTA
ASSISTING CHRISTIANS TO ACT
PUBLICATIONS

We Speak the Word of the Lord
A Practical Plan for More Effective Preaching
by Daniel E. Harris, C.M.

Edited by John Van Bemmel
Cover design by Tom A. Wright
Typesetting by Desktop Edit Shop, Inc.

Scripture quotes are taken from the *Lectionary for Mass. Vol. I: Sundays, Solemnities, Feasts of the Lord and the Saints* (New York: Catholic Book Publishing Company, 1998) or the *Lectionary for Mass* (New York: Catholic Book Publishing Company, 1970).

Published by: ACTA Publications
                Assisting Christians To Act
                4848 N. Clark Street
                Chicago, IL 60640-4711
                773-271-1030

Library of Congress Catalog Number: 200189152

ISBN: 0-87946-225-6

Printed in the United States of America

Year: 05 04 03 02 01
Printing: 7 6 5 4 3 2 1

Contents

Introduction

In the Footsteps of Eyewitnesses

The first gospel preachers were eyewitnesses. Their preaching, as reflected in the Christian scriptures, was characterized by its power and its simplicity. It introduced a dynamic new theology that is still developing. The strength of this new preaching was not based on its eloquence, its style or its theology. The first Christian preachers saw themselves as eyewitnesses called and sent. They emerged from the Pentecost experience on fire with the commission to preach the Christ they knew personally. These first preachers described their preaching ministry by declaring boldly, in the words of Peter: "[Jesus] went about doing good...for God was with him.... We are witness to all that he did.... He commissioned us to preach to the people...." (1 Peter 10:38,39,42).

The Need for Continuing Formation and Education

Professionals regularly make use of resources that keep them informed about developments in their field. Continuing education programs offer opportunities to hone skills in a particular area. Health professionals, teachers, lawyers, carpenters and other professionals and artisans read publications that keep them abreast of new developments. Conscientious professionals participate in conventions, seminars and workshops that allow them to interact with peers; they learn from others who have the same goals and vocation. This has not always been the case for Catholic preachers.

Until recently, preachers in the Catholic Church have had little opportunity for ongoing professional development. There are several reasons for this regrettable omission in our tradition. Before the Second Vatican Council, most seminaries did not offer systematic programs in homiletics. With few exceptions, students were simply expected to preach a few sermons for the faculty and students, often during the silent meals that were the norm in earlier days. Since preaching was not always taken seriously in the seminary, there was little interest in professional development once preachers were in active ministry.

We Speak the Word of the Lord is designed primarily for those who have had training in homiletics and are now engaged in active ministry. It addresses the special needs of Roman Catholic preachers, especially in their ministry of preaching the Sunday homily. It can be a valuable resource for seminarians engaged in homiletic training and for lay ministers in the Catholic tradition called to speak at prayer meetings, retreats, dedications and such occasions. Men and women in other faith traditions may also benefit from this book.

The Renewal of Preaching

In regard to the liturgy and preaching, the Catholic Church finds itself in a very different place since Vatican II. The Lectionary and the use of vernacular language in the liturgy have restored the scriptures to their place of prominence in worship. The topical sermon has been replaced by the Eucharistic homily that draws its message primarily from the Lectionary readings. Most seminaries and institutes of theology now provide solid homiletics programs that offer responsible training for both clergy and lay ministers.

This renewed interest in preaching has deepened the realization in ministers that homilies are not so much what a preacher does, as an expression of who a preacher is. The homily is the integrating point in ministry in the sense that what a preacher knows, believes and values are expressed to others in preaching. As ministers grow, their preaching will change and develop.

The recent explosion of information on the Internet offers preachers new opportunities for ongoing education and formation. Numerous sites feature an array of exegetical material and commentaries for each of the Sunday readings. Some sites present a variety of stories, quotes and personal reflections that help preachers connect with the congregations' everyday world. The same may be said of the books and periodicals on preaching published in recent years. (See the many entries in the Bibliography, pp. 207-213.) Preaching—by clerics and laity—is alive and flourishing in the information age.

Hunger for Preaching

Preachers may also find encouragement in knowing that there is a renewed hunger among people for the preached word. Parishioners have been known to "shop around" until they found a parish that offers better preaching, A few years ago, Aquinas Institute in St. Louis, Missouri, began presenting its "Preacher of the Year Award." In its first year, parishioners enthusiastically submitted nominations for consideration. None of the nominees were Chrysostoms or Augustines, but they were ministers who loved the word, loved to preach it and loved the people to whom they were sent to announce the good news. They preached in the down-to-earth language that named the presence of Christ in daily life. Congregations wanted these preachers recognized.

How to Use This Book

Preachers can use this book for private reading or as a resource for a peer-directed continuing education and formation group. As private reading, preachers will find affirmation in their ministry as well as challenges to explore fresh approaches to effective preaching. Even when this book is used for private study, readers will find it valuable to consult the Discussion Session Guidelines (pp. 193-205) to reflect on the questions posed for each chapter and to adapt the activities for their private use.

Readers can also use this book with other preachers. Many ministers have expressed a desire for increased opportunity to develop as preachers, but they find it increasingly difficult to devote the time needed to participate in formal continuing education programs. Others who may have the time for formal study find themselves geographically isolated from institutions that offer programs in preaching.

Using This Book with Groups (pp. 185-191) provides detailed guidelines for organizing a group process for preachers. It includes discussion questions, group activities and processes for offering feedback to fellow preachers. This peer-directed process is not intended to replace formal programs directed by homiletics professionals. Preachers may find it most useful as a way to build on their participation in a preaching workshop, such as Preaching the Just Word, offered by Walter Burghardt's team, or the Renewing Sunday Preaching convocations presented by the National Organization for Continuing Education of Roman Catholic Clergy (NOCERCC).

Does the Process Really Work?

After designing this peer-directed process, I established a pilot group in order to determine if this process would actually help preachers in their ministry. Would they invest themselves in the various discussions and activities? Would they be able to do quality work without a professional to guide them? I told the pilot group that as a silent observer I would simply note their interaction and progress. After observing a series of sessions, I was convinced that motivated preachers would benefit a great deal from participating in this type of experience. One of the volunteers later reported that it was the most valuable educational experience he had had since his ordination twenty years earlier. I would welcome hearing from any group that wishes to share its experience of this process. I welcome as well hearing from any individual whose preaching has improved from private use of this book.

Can We Really Enjoy Preaching?

I once concluded a seminary course in preaching by saying that I hoped the future ministers would enjoy preaching. One of the students nearly exploded in response, "Enjoy this! You didn't say we were supposed to enjoy this!" Perhaps we had spent too much time that semester stressing the hard work involved in writing and presenting effective homilies. It is hard work. But it is also life-giving work, which many ministers consider the most enjoyable aspect of their vocation.

This book, for private or group use, is meant to encourage preachers to step inside the scriptures with both feet, walk around in the world of the word, and step back out to preach the Christ they have met along their journey.

Chapter One

What Is a Homily?

Do We Preach Christ, or Preach *about* Christ?

Imagine this scene: It is Pentecost Sunday. The deacon has just proclaimed the magnificent gospel from John (20:19-23). It describes the resurrected Jesus breathing the Holy Spirit on the frightened disciples, giving them the power to leave their place of hiding and fearlessly preach the word. After the gospel, the preacher approaches the pulpit and begins the homily:

> My dear people of God, the *Catechism of the Catholic Church* (n. 1287) tells us that the Holy Spirit, given on the day of Pentecost, gave the apostles the power to proclaim the message of Christ and call people to baptism. Part of this baptism, the next article tells us, included a laying on of hands that became what we now call the sacrament of confirmation. As the catechism continues, we learn that an anointing with perfumed oil (chrism) was added to the laying on of hands. Soon our own parish school children will receive this great sacrament. This seems an excellent opportunity to explain what our catechism teaches about this sacrament of confirmation....

Is this an authentic homily? The preacher is talking about the Holy Spirit and using an authoritative source to explain doctrine, but does that make it a homily? Many contemporary Catholics are frankly ignorant of what the church teaches. Would the homily, then, not be an opportune time to present some good old-fashioned instruction? There are those who want the homily to be a time for a program of solid, systematic catechesis from the pulpit. Would a catechetical talk at the pulpit during the Eucharist still be a homily?

1. The Many Faces of Preaching

The term "preaching" incorporates a wide variety of ways to proclaim the words and deeds of God. It includes forms—including Christian witness—that may not require spoken words at all. The *Code of Canon Law* (nn. 756-70) speaks of the "Ministry of the Divine Word" shared by all the people of God by virtue of their baptism. Jesus continues to call every believer to proclaim the message he gave his first followers. Through word and example, Christians are called to spread the good news where they live, work and play. Missionaries who bring the gospel to the most remote areas of the world preach the word of God. So do retreat directors, leaders in religious communities of men and women, elementary school teachers, parents. All of their activity to communicate the word of God can rightly be called preaching in the broadest sense, and in some instances this will involve teaching as well as preaching. *We Speak the Word of the Lord* does not attempt to deal with these various faces of preaching, important as they are. Nor does it deal with catechesis. This book is focused on a unique form of preaching, the Eucharistic homily.

The Homily As a Unique Form of Preaching

The homily has a specific function in the believing community. Because the homily is part of the liturgy itself, it celebrates the presence of God here and now active in the lives of believers. The homily does not merely talk *about* God. It is, rather, an experience of the personal presence of God as the church worships.

Not all preaching uttered from pulpits is homiletical. A "homily" is preaching on the scripture readings of the day. Preaching within the Eucharist has had a long and varied history. In our own time, the Roman Catholic Church has been rediscovering the richness of the liturgical homily. A careful reading of official statements concerning preaching reveals, however, that the church's understanding of the liturgical homily is still developing.[1] The question is not merely an academic one. The preacher's very identity as a minister of the word is at stake.

The following preaching samples illustrate why the issue is a vital one. We need only consider a brief section of each homily to appreciate how vastly different the two approaches are. Both examples are based on the story of the prodigal son (Luke 15:11-32). In these samples, is the preacher merely talking about God and what God expects, or is the preacher allowing the listener to encounter God?

Preaching Sample 1

Persons who are addicted to alcohol or drugs usually report the experience they call hitting bottom. They reach a point where they suddenly realize they have fallen into a sorry state and cannot pull themselves back up. It is then that they can begin the healing process. The young man in this story we have just heard also had an experience of hitting bottom. He was not in the grip of chemical dependency, however. He was in the grip of sin. He turned against his father and his homeland. He chose a reckless life of sin and now he had hit bottom. He wanted to go back home where life was secure. His situation is a powerful reminder that you and I need to turn back to God when we have sinned.

This gospel presents an excellent opportunity to reflect on the fact that some of us would excuse every sinful act by calling it the result of a wounded childhood. The truth is that sin is a reality and that people choose to sin. The *Catechism of the Catholic Church* reminds us that mortal sin is a serious offense and deprives us of God's kingdom if the sin is unrepented and therefore not forgiven. Let us consider the conditions that make a sin mortal and what we are to do if we have sinned seriously. The Catechism defines mortal sin as...

Preaching Sample 2

At first this appears to be a beautiful story about a wayward son who finally came to his senses and repented. Is that all that this gospel is saying? Did you notice that the prodigal son was far more concerned about his own sorry state than about what he did to his father? He realized he had given up a rather good life back on the farm. Did you also notice that he rehearsed a very moving speech? "Father, I have sinned against heaven and against you. I no longer deserve to be called your son; treat me as you would treat one of your hired workers." We hear him later trying to rattle off that pitiful speech word for word just as he had practiced it. It does not look as if he was really sorry at all. And the poor foolish father turned this kid into the hero of the hour, killing even a precious fatted calf for a party! How is the boy ever going to learn to grow up if his father does not teach him that behavior has certain consequences?

I once read this story to a group of poor children, most of whom came from homes without loving fathers. They had never heard the story. When I got to the part about the father seeing the son coming down the road, I stopped reading and asked the children what they thought the father should do. One of the little children said, "The father's gonna' beat the tar outta him!" Most of the children agreed that is what would happen, or at least that is what should happen if the father is going to act in any normal way. When I continued reading the story, the children seemed shocked that the father foolishly heaped such tender love on the son who had hurt him so badly. What is Jesus telling us about God our Father?

Homily or Sermon?

These are two very different approaches to the gospel story. Both examples present the truth in a clear, straightforward way. But are both authentic homilies? To answer that question, it will be necessary to define a homily. The first sample suggests a catechetical preaching event that instructs Catholics on the doctrines of sin and forgiveness. If the preaching were to continue on that level, the listeners would get a clear idea of what the church expects them to believe and do about sin and the confession of sin. That type of instruction would be one good way to deal with these issues in an RCIA session, but it does not fit the guidelines for a liturgical homily.

Since the Second Vatican Council (1962-65), the church has called for homilies within the Eucharist. Some Catholic preachers continue to ask, "What is the difference between a sermon and a homily?" Preaching Sample 1 is an example of a sermon, which is a preaching event based on any source or topic the preacher chooses. It need not be based on the liturgical readings. It also may serve a variety of purposes, including catechesis or moral exhortation. There are many appropriate places for sermons in the church's life, but they do not belong within the Eucharist. It is important to note that Catholics and Protestants do not mean the same thing when they use the word "sermon" to describe preaching. Protestants use the word to describe most forms of worship preaching. To further complicate the issue, some Catholic documents do not make clear distinctions between sermons and homilies.

2. Historical Struggles

The nature and purpose of the liturgical homily are not new issues for the church. During certain times in its history, the church witnessed notions of preaching that seem very strange today, including a papal decree mandating that two-hour sermons should henceforth be limited to thirty minutes. There was even a time in the sixteenth century when children preached to the pope![2] It goes beyond the purpose of this book to offer even a cursory history of preaching and the many struggles over the definition of preaching within public worship. As interesting as that history is, a more important question for contemporary ministers is, "What does the church expect of those called to authentically preach the word of God to believers gathered for Eucharist?"

One pivotal moment in the long history of that question, and one that sheds light on where we are today, took place at the time of Martin Luther. Central to his conflict with church authorities that eventually led to the Protestant Reformation was his passion for authentic liturgical preaching. His insistence that Jesus Christ be preached would be quite at home among movements in the contemporary Catholic Church to rediscover the essence of the liturgical homily.

Martin Luther and the First Homily Helps

Luther was appalled that the preachers of his time were concerned with moralistic talks devoid of the saving power of Jesus Christ. He took great pains to carefully instruct his followers on how to plumb the depths of the scriptures and present the person of Christ in the preached word. He wrote a number of *postils* that contained these detailed directives.[3] The postils characteristically illustrated the kernel of the gospel rather than concern themselves with mere teaching on dogmas or morals. They served as detailed guides for preaching a sound liturgical homily that proclaimed Jesus Christ.

What does Luther's care in preparing the postils for the preachers of his day say to contemporary preachers? One issue seems immediately obvious. He was convinced that the sermon (contemporary Catholics would use the term "homily") emerged from the presence of Christ in the scriptures rather than from doctrines or morals on which the preacher may wish to expound. It is crucial that the church teach sound doctrines and morals, but that is not the purpose of the homily. The Eucharistic homily is a special time when the people of God gather for a unique experience of encountering God in the living word. It is not mere instruction.

3. Rediscovering the Homily

The church in our own time has emerged from a long history of understanding the sermon to be a time of instruction. Because the church felt it must guard itself against the ideas of the Protestant Reformation, a great deal of emphasis was placed on explaining doctrine from the pulpit. In the American church, for example, "the Baltimore Fathers seem to relegate Holy Scripture to a place subsidiary to formal Christian doctrine."[4] For too long, preachers have used the time after the gospel reading merely to explain how people should behave as Christians. All too rarely in our recent history have preachers proclaimed the very person of Christ present in the liturgy. More recent statements from the American bishops have called preachers to a renewed understanding of the liturgical homily in light of the Second Vatican Council.

Church Documents and Preaching
The official documents of the Roman Catholic Church do not all agree on one, clear definition of the Eucharistic homily. At times the documents describe the homily as an experience of God's presence. At other times, preachers are encouraged to use the homily as

a vehicle to teach doctrine.

The *Constitution on the Sacred Liturgy*, for example, calls the homily, "a proclamation of God's wonderful works in the history of salvation, which is the mystery of Christ ever made present and active in us, especially in the celebration of the liturgy" (n. 35). This stands in contrast to the way preaching is described in the *Catechism of the Catholic Church*, which equates liturgical preaching with instruction. The catechism describes the liturgy as, "the privileged place for catechizing the People of God" (n. 1017).

Robert Waznak, writing in *America*, warns that equating a homily with catechesis conflicts with Vatican II's emphasis on the liturgical homily as a moment of worship, an experience of the mystery of Christ. He quotes *Fulfilled in Your Hearing*, which states that the homilist is not primarily a teacher and the liturgy is not primarily concerned with catechesis.[5] This confusion over the relationship between the homily and catechesis takes on added significance in light of various movements to produce a syllabus of preaching topics for each Sunday of the year. The church needs to discover creative ways to teach sound doctrine and morals, but it would be tragic if preachers replaced authentic liturgical preaching from the scriptures with religious and moral instruction.

The National Conference of Catholic Bishops requested its Committee on Priestly Life and Ministry to explore the nature and purpose of the liturgical homily. In 1982 the committee produced *Fulfilled in Your Hearing: The Homily in the Sunday Assembly*.[6] The document has been a valuable contribution, offering practical guidelines to preachers at a time when the church is taking a new look at the role of preaching within the Eucharist. The document is especially helpful in distinguishing the characteristics of the liturgical homily as a unique form of the much broader category called preaching. The term "preaching" can refer to such wide-ranging moments as pre-evangelization aimed at those who do not yet believe, evangelization that calls believers to a conversion of heart, and catechesis that teaches doctrine and morals (*Fulfilled*, nn. 26-27). This document helps to dispel potential confusion among the many types of preaching by describing a homily in terms of its particular source, purpose and style.

Source: The Scriptures

Before the Second Vatican Council, it was common for preachers to choose sermon topics based on the needs of the congregation or the preacher's own interests. In some places, preachers followed a sermon topic outline intended to cover a series of themes throughout the year. These talks were often moral exhortations or catechesis. Sermons were usually interruptions in the liturgy. *Fulfilled in Your Hearing* calls for preaching from the scriptures, not from sermon topics.

Besides emphasizing the scriptures as the source for liturgical homilies, the document describes how preachers are to bring the congregation into contact with God's word. Preaching a homily is not a process of using the scriptures to instruct an unbelieving world. The process is the other way around: The homily brings people's lives to the scriptures:

> The homily is not so much *on* the Scriptures as *from* them and *through* them.... Since the purpose of the homily is to enable the gathered congregation to celebrate the liturgy with faith, the preacher does not so much attempt to explain the Scriptures as to interpret the human situation through the Scriptures (*Fulfilled*, n. 20).

Purpose: Faith, Not Instruction

The document describes the homily as a special type of preaching that goes beyond instruction. It derives its character from being "a part of the liturgy itself" (*Constitution on the Sacred Liturgy*, n. 52). The purpose of the homily is to proclaim the scriptures read at the liturgy so that the congregation will be able to celebrate in faith (*Fulfilled*, n. 17). The homily is therefore not simply an action within the liturgy, it *is* liturgy. As liturgy, it does not merely instruct or exhort; it helps the congregation to worship.

Even since Vatican II, some published works have advocated "preaching syllabi," or master sermon plans that outline a series of preaching themes based on the Lectionary readings. Groups with special agendas have provided homily outlines that draw themes from the scriptures or other liturgical sources. These programs miss the central issue: The homily has a purpose. Basing the preaching on the prescribed Lectionary readings does not necessarily make the event a homily. As part of the liturgy, the homily must lead to faith and a deeper participation in the Eucharist. It is not simply to offer information or instruction.

Style: Conversational

The third characteristic that distinguishes the homily from other forms of preaching is its unique style. In recent church history, the study of homiletics was often called Sacred Eloquence. Unfortunately, homilies and sermons were sometimes pompous affairs designed to showcase the preacher's oratorical skills. *Fulfilled in Your Hearing* returns to the ancient notion of a homily as preaching that employs familiar, conversational language. Good homiletic style avoids vague, abstract and impersonal language in favor of simple, concrete language that speaks to the experience of the faithful. On the other hand, because preaching is worship, the style is never chatty or trivial (*Fulfilled*, nn. 23-24).

This is one of the few instances in which a church document suggests a style for preaching. The documents of the Second Vatican Council and subsequent statements on the homily speak about its scriptural sources, its purpose and its relation to the Eucharist. Rarely is the Catholic preacher given direction about the style of a homily. A later chapter that deals with the qualities of outstanding homilies will explore appropriate style in greater detail.

First-Order and Second-Order Language

For now, we will limit the discussion of style to one observation concerning language. A preacher's understanding of the liturgical homily has consequences for the kind of language the preacher uses. Since a homily is about preaching the faith of the church rather than simply explaining its doctrine, the appropriate language of preaching is what M. C. Hilkert calls *first-order language*, the language that speaks not only to the listeners' understanding, but to their lived faith experience.

Speaking as a theologian, Hilkert observes that the disciplines of preaching and theology employ their own proper type of language in communicating the same mystery of God. Preaching, the Bible and the liturgy employ first-order language that speaks to the whole realm of human experience on its many levels of emotion as well as reason. Theology, which is *second-order language*, is designed to "provide limits for the imagination, rather than to evoke the community's religious experience."[7]

Although the language of preaching intended to evoke experience is different from the language of theology, good preaching is theologically and scripturally sound. Skillful preachers integrate their scholarship with their faith as they proclaim the message in the language of lived experience. Consider the following examples.

Example: Second-Order Language of Theology

The Virgin Mary, who at the message of the angel received the word of God in her heart and in her body and gave Life to the world, is acknowledged and honored as being truly the Mother of God and of the redeemer. Redeemed, in a more exalted fashion, by reason of the merits of her Son and united to him by a close and indissoluble tie, she is endowed with the high office and dignity of the Mother of the Son of God, and therefore she is also the beloved daughter of the Father and the temple of the Holy Spirit (*Dogmatic Constitution on the Church*, n. 53).

Example: First-Order Language of Preaching

She was young. Mary was a Jewish girl about fifteen years old, engaged to Joseph the tradesman. Like other young women in her time she knew where her place would be. She would be confined to the home. She would not be permitted to speak in public or gather in public places where the men could freely meet to swap stories or engage in business. Mary really was a nobody in the eyes of many people in her hometown. But God saw Mary very differently. God chose this woman to be the mother of Jesus.

Homilies Focus on God, Not on Ourselves

It may sound obvious to say that homilies proclaim God. Surprisingly, preachers often center attention solely on the believers and what they are expected to do. Look back for a moment at the two preaching samples based on the prodigal son early in this chapter. Beyond what they illustrate about the differences between teaching and preaching, the examples also differ greatly in their subjects.

The first example quickly centers attention on what the congregation should know, believe and do as Catholics. If the preaching were to continue in this direction, it would probably go on to develop various issues centering on the believers' responsibilities. As important as that message is for preaching in its wider sense, it is not the subject for a liturgical homily.

The second example, on the other hand, allows the listeners to meet a forgiving God by focusing attention on the prodigal son's merciful father. Put another way, the first preacher was speaking *on* the scriptures, the second preacher was speaking *from* the scriptures. The *Constitution on the Sacred Liturgy* reminds preachers that a homily:

> ...should draw its content mainly from scriptural and liturgical sources, for it is the proclamation of God's wonderful works in the history of salvation, which is the mystery of Christ, ever made present and active in us, especially in the celebration of the liturgy (n. 35).

Even though *Fulfilled in Your Hearing*, as noted earlier, calls preachers to interpret human experience in light of the scriptures, homilies do not stop at giving advice and directives for good Christian living. Many persons, more qualified than preachers, are able to offer good advice. Homilies offer something that advice cannot give: They bring the believer and God into each other's presence.

Preaching As a Personal Experience of God
Preaching is not so much talking about God as it is a personal encounter among God, the congregation and the preacher. As one of the earliest Christian preachers realized in 1 Thessalonians. 2:13: "And for this reason we too give thanks to God unceasingly, that, in receiving the word of God from hearing us, you received not a human word but, as it truly is, the word of God, which is now at work in you who believe." This special encounter is sometimes described as "breaking open the word." The image suggests an interactive experience, in which the believer is invited to meet the Lord in faith.

Karl Rahner notes that as important as doctrine is, it can only talk *about* God. Doctrine does not bring the listener into personal contact with God. In contrast, the word spoken within the celebration of the Eucharist "is the salutary word which brings with it what it affirms. It is itself therefore salvific event...and brings about what it displays. It renders the grace of God present."[8]

Preaching is a unique type of communication in that the speaker is not in full control of the listeners' response. Salespersons, lecturers, teachers, therapists or other professional communicators can achieve their goals of selling vacuum cleaners, imparting information or healing psyches, provided they can skillfully shape a message that employs just the right rhetorical strategies to achieve their desired purpose in the listener. Preaching, on the other hand, has its own internal power to move hearts. The power comes not from carefully crafted rhetoric, but from the word itself. The preached word has its own dynamic power to bring faith, heal troubled souls and move the believer to action. This means that the preachers too, not just the people in the pew, are "under the word." The homily has the power to bring good news to the preachers in ways they may not have intended when they carefully prepared their message. The preached word contains its own power.

4. Can Homilies Teach?

At this point, preachers may be wondering whether or not it is ever proper to teach the faithful during a homily. While it is more appropriate to offer instruction in those preaching events that involve catechesis, such as the RCIA, missionary preaching or pre-evangelization settings, the homily is a special time for proclaiming rather than explaining. As Robert Lechner notes, "It must intend not just information but transformation."[9] Sometimes it is necessary to teach in order for authentic preaching to take place. At times a preacher will need to explain unfamiliar details from the very different world of ancient cultures found in the scriptures. At other times certain difficult ideas may need a few words of theological precision if the preacher is to be faithful in proclaiming an accurate message. In determining how much time to allot for instruction, good preachers teach only enough to help proclaim the scriptures. The following comments on the account of the cure of Bartimaeus illustrate how teaching can aid proclamation.

> As [Jesus] was leaving Jericho with his disciples and a
> sizable crowd, Bartimaeus, a blind man, the son of
> Timaeus, sat by the roadside begging. On hearing that it
> was Jesus of Nazareth, he began to cry out and say,
> "Jesus, son of David, have pity on me." And many
> rebuked him, telling him to be silent. But he kept calling
> out all the more, "Son of David, have pity on me." Jesus
> stopped and said, "Call him." So they called the blind
> man, saying to him, "Take courage; get up, Jesus is call-
> ing you." He threw aside his cloak, sprang up, and came
> to Jesus. Jesus said to him in reply, "What do you want
> me to do for you?" The blind man replied to him, "Mas-
> ter, I want to see." Jesus told him, "Go your way; your
> faith has saved you." Immediately he received his sight
> and followed him on the way.
>
> Mark 10:46-52

Teaching That Aids Proclamation

On the surface it seems obvious how the homily based on this miracle will develop. This story shows Jesus as one with the power to heal physical blindness and, by implication, to heal all that afflicts people. The homily will most likely be about the power of Jesus. Preachers might ask if there is more going on here. If preach-ers investigate the cultural notions of healing in Jesus' time, they will discover that the evangelist has a far richer message than might first appear.

Physical blindness is an expression of spiritual blindness, of inner dullness. This is a complex notion for modern Western peo-ple. We tend to freely vocalize our inner thoughts and feelings, as we can see on countless afternoon television talk shows where char-acters pour out their every thought and emotion for the camera. The biblical authors and their original audiences lacked the sense of self that allowed them to think in terms that correspond to our cat-egories of self-consciousness. First-century eastern Mediterranean people used external zones of the body to express inner realities. For them, it made little sense to say, "You must think carefully about what I am telling you. Let it sink into your mind." It is another thing to ask them, "Do you *see* it?" For these ancients, the eyes were the special zones of the body that corresponded to emotion-fused thought. The zones involving the hands and feet as well as the ears and mouth also involved inner realities that we moderns can describe with a vocabulary unknown to the people of Jesus' time.[10]

Preaching about Healing Stories

When preachers deal with healing stories that involve the zone of the eyes, they can be certain that the text is discussing more than a misfortune afflicting a part of the physical body. As Jesus heals the blind, they are also healed to know, understand and choose Jesus as the one who can truly bring them God's grace. When Jesus heals the deaf or speech impaired, they are now also healed to take in the good news, the efficacious word of God. They are also empowered to guard against impurities entering and leaving their person, since the mouth and ears are the body orifices that maintain purity and a sense of status quo for the believer. Preachers who note healing stories in the zone of the mouth and ears are dealing with the hearing and proclamation of the good news of Jesus. The zone of hands and feet is the zone of purposeful activity. Healing stories involving this zone tell the reader more than incidents of healed limbs. The healed are now free to act. These healings may involve a person being healed to follow Jesus not just physically, but with their whole person. After Jesus healed the sick person carried to him on a mat, he commanded the man to pick up his mat and walk. He was to walk with renewed purpose as a believer.

Would it be helpful for the preacher to present all the details of first-century Mediterranean notions of how the three physical zones allow the people of the Bible to express inner realities? Obviously, that discussion is better left to the Bible study group. On the other hand, can the homily proclaim what Jesus is doing for Bartimaeus if preachers totally ignore the fruits of scholarship? The following segment of a homily illustrates one strategy for teaching just enough to allow the proclamation.

Example: Teaching That Aids Proclamation

The bystanders who witnessed this healing saw something you and I probably did not see. Like us, they saw that someone who had been physically blind could now see by the power of Jesus. This is a wonderful miracle, of course. But the people of Jesus' time saw more than meets our eyes.

You young people here today who are in school have probably heard your math teachers tell you repeatedly, "Think about this problem. Use your head. Put on your thinking caps." We know that to grasp a difficult problem we must mull it over in our brains, we must weigh all the details. But the people of Jesus' time would have had no idea what we were talking about. For them to really grasp an issue meant they had to *see* it. To use the eyes was to understand, to believe. They would not say, "Think about it." They would say, "Look at it. See it."

When Jesus opened the eyes of Bartimaeus he was really allowing the beggar to see him as Lord, to believe in his heart that this man Jesus was more than meets the eye. Bartimaeus was given the eyes of faith. He could see Jesus.

This segment from the beginning of a homily on the healing story employs just enough teaching to set the groundwork for a homily that can develop into one that proclaims Jesus who calls us to believe. The brief instruction is not an end in itself but a means to aid the preaching. Too much instruction would result in the congregation merely understanding a complex cultural insight about physical healing. To ignore this issue would mean that the richness of the scriptures might have been lost.

Defining a Homily

The Second Vatican Council and *Fulfilled in Your Hearing* have refocused the church's attention on the special characteristics of the liturgical homily. The church calls preachers to root the homily in the scriptures as the source of the message. In some instances, the documents declare that a homily proclaims the mighty words and works of God rather than simply offers instruction. In others, the documents are ambivalent on this issue of proclamation and instruction. It is not always clear whether the documents are speaking about preaching in general, or the liturgical homily in particular.[11] A precise definition of the liturgical homily is still in progress.

This chapter began with the question, "What is a homily?" We are at a time in the church when it may be premature to say there is one precise definition. The scriptures themselves do not provide any one definitive image of God, but reveal a God of many faces. Perhaps the church's understanding of a homily must also resist precise limits. Considering the many fresh insights the church has expressed about the nature and purpose of the liturgical homily since the Second Vatican Council, the following definition can serve as a guide for ministers of the word as they preach and as they call one another to better preaching:

> A homily is a preaching event that is integral to the liturgy to proclaim the saving mystery of God in the scriptures. It calls and empowers the hearers to faith, a deeper participation in the Eucharist, and daily discipleship to Christ lived out in the church.

The Identity of the Preacher

This definition is not intended to capture all that can be said about the liturgical homily. It is offered as a working definition to provide direction for the reader and individual preachers to reflect on their own homilies, and for those using the peer-directed formation group, described in the appendix, to discuss and appraise the homilies presented by group members. The mystery of God working in the lives of people cannot be exhausted in a few words. The following insight on the identity of a preacher from one of the earliest Christians suggests how limitless preaching must necessarily be:

> What was from the beginning,
> what we have heard,
> what we have seen with our eyes,
> what we have looked upon
> and have touched with our hands
> concerns the Word of life...
> what we have seen and heard
> we proclaim now to you....

> 1 John 1:1,3

Further Reading

The Bishops' Committee on Priestly Life and Ministry, National Conference of Catholic Bishops, *Fulfilled in Your Hearing: The Homily in the Sunday Assembly*. Washington, D.C.: United States Catholic Conference, 1982.

Harris, Daniel, and Edward Murphy. "What Is a Homily?" In *Overtaken By the Word: The Theology and Practice of Preaching*. Denver: Rubicon, 1990.

Pilla, Anthony. "Ministry of the Word." *Origins* 25 (1995): 277-87.

Waznak, Robert P. "Homily." In *The New Dictionary of Sacramental Worship*. Edited by Peter E. Fink. Collegeville, Minn.: Liturgical Press, 1990, pp. 552-58.

Notes

1. Robert P. Waznak, "Homily," in *The New Dictionary of Sacramental Worship*, ed. Peter E. Fink (Collegeville, Minn.: Liturgical Press, 1990), pp. 552-58.

2. John W. O'Malley, *Praise and Blame in Renaissance Rome: Rhetoric, Doctrine and Reform in the Sacred Orators of the Papal Courts*, c. 1450-1521 (Durham, N.C.: Duke University Press, 1979), pp. 23-26.

3. The term comes from Luther's standard way of starting a scriptural sermon. From the Latin phrase, *"post illa verba sacrae scripturae," post illa* was the shortened phrase by which people popularly referred to this type of expository sermon. See Fred W. Mueser, *Luther the Preacher* (Minneapolis: Augsburg, 1983), p. 37.

4. Robert F. McNamara, *Catholic Sunday Preaching: The American Guidelines—1791-1975* (Special Study Series) (Washington, D.C.: Word of God Institute, 1975), p. 22.

5. Robert P. Waznak, "The Catechism and the Sunday Homily," *America*, 22 October 1994, 19.

6. The Bishops' Committee on Priestly Life and Ministry, National Conference of Catholic Bishops, *Fulfilled in Your Hearing: The Homily in the Sunday Assembly* (Washington, D.C.: United States Catholic Conference, 1982).

7. Mary Catherine Hilkert, *Naming Grace: Preaching and the Sacramental Imagination* (New York: Continuum, 1997), p. 132.

8. Karl Rahner, "The Word and the Eucharist," in *Theological Investigations* IV, trans. Kevin Smyth (Baltimore: Helicon Press, 1966), p. 260.

9. Robert Lechner, "Liturgical Preaching," *Worship* 37 (1962-63): 640.

10. Bruce J. Malina, "Eyes-Heart," in *Biblical Social Values and Their Meanings: A Handbook*, ed. John J. Pilch and Bruce J. Malina (Peabody, Mass.: Hendrickson, 1993), p. 64.

11. Waznak, "Homily," p. 557.

Chapter Two

Making a Homily Outstanding

Can Every Homily Be Outstanding?

Chapter One posed the question, "What is a homily?" It examined the theological and liturgical elements that make the homily a unique type of preaching. This chapter asks, "What makes a homily outstanding?" Of course, strictly speaking, not every homily can be outstanding (if every homily is, then none are), but we'll use this word to describe those homilies that possess the eight qualities explained below, the qualities required for an effective homily. So, what does a really good homily look like?

Is it fair to expect all homilies to be outstanding? In the sense we are using the word and as we describe the eight qualities that homilies should possess, yes! Can every preacher be another Chrysostom, an Augustine, a Luther, or a Martin Luther King, Jr.? No, not all preachers living today will be remembered among the great ones of history, or perhaps even remembered by their contemporaries. Nor do all preachers share equal gifts of eloquence, which, after all, may be only one feature of an outstanding preacher.

The people of God have a right to outstanding homilies. In *On Evangelization in the Modern World*, Pope Paul VI describes the qualities that should characterize every Eucharistic homily. He says that the faithful expect preaching that is:

> ...simple, clear, direct, well-adapted, profoundly dependent on Gospel teaching and faithful to the magisterium, animated by a balanced apostolic ardor coming from its own characteristic nature, full of hope, fostering belief, and productive of peace and unity (n. 43).

1. Qualities of an Outstanding Homily

The following eight qualities of an outstanding homily challenge preachers to respond to what Paul VI maintains believers need to nourish their lives and therefore have a right to expect. Many preaching experts have suggested norms for outstanding preaching. Catherine LaCugna, for example, lists five basic principles in the article recommended in Further Reading at the end of this chapter (p. 43). The following criteria reflect the opinions of some of these preaching authorities. This list also reflects the practical benefits I have gleaned from striving for over twenty-five years to preach outstanding homilies, and from listening to thousands of students and ministers who have preached outstanding, and sometimes less than outstanding, homilies. Because individual preachers possess different gifts, some will excel in all these areas, while others will struggle with some of them. Despite this variety of gifts and talents, all ministers of the word are called to outstanding preaching characterized by these criteria. Such attributes distinguish a homily from the all too commonplace and ordinary; they are the qualities that prompt people to comment, "I really liked that homily today."

A. Proclaims the Scriptures

As noted in the previous chapter, we preach a homily *from* the scriptures, not merely *on* the scriptures. An outstanding homily means that preachers spend serious time praying and studying the word. They have gone the extra step of wrestling with the word and allowing it to engage their faith. John Heil describes the process in which readers interact with the scriptures to produce meaning. They allow the text to engage them not simply on the level of abstract assent, but on the richer level of images, feelings and attitudes. In this exchange, readers will be sensitive to what the text *does* to them and how it *affects* them.[1]

When preachers immerse themselves in the text, allowing the word to challenge them on many levels, it is more likely that the homily will focus attention on the presence of God in the word. If preachers simply take a cursory look at the readings, the result is often a talk that merely explains a theme or topic. A catechetical talk on the parable of the Prodigal Son, for example, might describe our need for conversion. A liturgical homily on the same gospel proclaims the God who unconditionally forgives sinners. The first approach centers only on the believer's responsibility. The second focuses on the person of God. Homilies, as already noted, will contain elements of teaching, even sermonizing. *The Constitution on the Sacred Liturgy*, though, reminds preachers that the primary focus of the homily is "the proclamation of God's wonderful works...which is the mystery of Christ" (n. 35.2.). Chapter Four deals in greater detail with preaching the scriptures.

B. Witnesses the Faith

In an outstanding homily the word of a believer witnesses faith to other believers. When Jesus preached in the synagogue for the first time, he spoke about how he experienced the word of God, as recorded by Isaiah, in his own life. When Jesus finished reading the text he announced, "Today this scripture passage is fulfilled in your hearing" (Luke 4:21). His first disciples continued this tradition of witnessing by preaching the Christ they *knew*, not simply the Christ they knew *about*. Robert Maloney, Superior General of the Congregation of the Mission, wrote to his preachers:

> It is most important that we ourselves experience the love God reveals through the cross, that we have a deep confidence in a personal loving God who works actively in our lives. This is the foundation for all our preaching and for all our pastoral ministry. Our own experience of God's love will move us to proclaim it as good news.[2]

In the footsteps of Jesus and the apostles, contemporary homilists witness to their faith; they do not just explain their faith. Other forms of preaching call for catechesis and even apologetics. The liturgical homily, as an act of worship, is the time for proclaiming the person of God. Walter Burghardt cautions preachers that they risk irrelevancy if they do not preach the God they know personally. Merely teaching about God is not enough because, "if you know only a theology of God, not the God of theology, you will not be the preacher our world desperately needs."[3]

Some homiletic authorities warn preachers never to talk about themselves in a homily. Others say explicit personal witness is the most effective way to proclaim the word. Whether, in a homily, preachers talk explicitly about their personal faith is not the issue. Outstanding homilies focus attention on God's word, not on the preacher's life. The way preachers talk about their faith is the issue. Authentic witnessing does not leave the congregation impressed with the holiness of the preacher. It helps the congregation see God at work in one believer's life. A preacher is merely being self-indulgent in talking about "my God." A preacher is witnessing in talking about, "*my* God." Walter Burghardt notes:

> There is a delicate line between the "I" that incites the reaction "Ah yes" that stirs the listeners to think and tell their own story, and the "I" that embarrasses, that makes others mumble uncomfortably, "I'm sorry for your troubles, Father."[4]

Authentic witnessing need not be limited to the preacher's personal faith experience. Since homilies profess the faith of the church, not a preacher's private faith, witness preaching is also an appropriate time to include other voices in the homily. Preachers also act as witnesses when they allow the faith stories of other believers to speak. Chapter Six, "Listening to the Listeners," deals with how to include other voices in the homily.

C. Is Imaginative

Chapter One quoted *Fulfilled in Your Hearing*: "[T]he preacher does not so much attempt to explain the Scriptures as to interpret the human situation through the Scriptures" (n. 20). The scriptures interpret the wonderful works of God among God's people by appealing to images, metaphors, analogies and the whole gamut of sights, sounds and smells that make up real life. Preachers do an injustice to God's word if they take refuge in abstract theological formulas. Interpreting the human situation requires using the language of the human situation.

Jesus proclaimed the scriptures by interpreting them in terms of the human situation. His many parables and example stories feature earthy images and everyday life experiences. His preaching mentioned fig trees, mustard seeds, lost sheep and coins, a jealous older brother, and a woman who is busy in the kitchen while her sister sits at the master's feet. Those who preach in Jesus' name today will search for fresh ways to interpret the word by careful observation of the contemporary human situation.

Consider these two approaches to the story in which Jesus curses a barren fig tree when he sought its fruit (Matthew 21:18-22):

Example: Abstract Language

At first glance, Jesus seems somewhat vindictive and capricious in cursing the fig tree. The incident harkens back to images of the ancient prophets upbraiding their people for their empty piety. The people were quick to follow the prescripts of formal religion, but their lives did not reflect the type of good works that characterize true believers.

Example: Imaginative Language

Last week I saw a barren fig tree. Have you ever seen one? I was at a nature preserve featuring exotic shrubs and trees. Most of them were green and full of life. Then I came upon the barren fig tree. It stood so starkly that at first I thought it was an artificial decoration. There was no sign that it had ever lived or ever would live. Fig trees, the plaque at the base said, go through barren phases. What a powerful image of the person who has shut out the life of God!

Preachers sometimes ask where they can find good stories and concrete images for their homilies. There are collections of homily stories and illustrations in print, in computer versions of homily helps, and even on the Internet. Preachers may be tempted to rush too quickly to these canned sources during the homily preparation process. Borrowing too often from prepared homily resources can cause preachers to become mere eavesdroppers on others who have interpreted the scriptures through their own life experiences. A preacher's own faith journey is often the most fruitful source for concrete homily material.

D. Is Hopeful

This chapter began with an appeal from Paul VI for lively preaching filled with apostolic hope. Outstanding preaching does not dwell on how sinners constantly fail to live the gospel. Instead, it encourages a pilgrim people to continue the journey despite inevitable failures.

Some preachers find it easy to paint vivid images of what is wrong with the world. They struggle to find equally concrete language to describe what life can be like for those who love God and one another. Newspapers, radio and television provide a continuous supply of stories that graphically detail murders, child pornography and spousal abuse. Preachers too often devote a large section of the homily to pointing out these evils only to conclude with a brief and usually weak appeal to love one another. One priest who worked with youth observed that ministers are good at telling young Christians they cannot steal, lie, cheat or engage in sex outside of marriage. They are clear and specific in warning youth that Christ does not allow these activities. Are preachers equally vocal in proclaiming what young people are free to do and be, once Christ has entered their lives?

Homilies of hope rejoice in the full life that Jesus promises to those who remain faithful through their lifelong pilgrim journey. Because this quality of preaching is best expressed through witness, homilies of hope narrate stories of those who have begun to live that promise in this life. Preachers who are sustained by the power of Christ in their lives will be eager to tell others about the hope that strengthens them in their perseverance. They will not be afraid to admit that they have sometimes failed. One of the greatest preachers of all time finally came to rejoice in the hopeful conviction that "when I am weak, then I am strong" (2 Corinthians 12:10).

E. Is in Touch with People's Lives

There is nothing quite as boring as a lengthy answer to a question that the listener has not really asked. Outstanding homilies are in touch with the faith experiences of those in the congregation. People come to the Eucharist with questions that need answers, with hurts that need healing, with loneliness that needs filling and, thankfully, with joys that need to be expressed in prayer and song and preaching. Henri Nouwen calls creative preachers to be in touch with people's faith lives by maintaining a spirit of *dialogue*. This dialogue is not a mere technique, but an attitude in which preachers allow themselves to be vulnerable through continual involvement in the lives of their people.[5] Some of Jesus' contemporaries criticized him for dining with sinners. They may have felt that a truly holy person must stand apart and above the unclean masses. Preachers who want to be in touch with their congregations cannot afford to isolate themselves from the everyday concerns of the people.

Anthony Pilla, Bishop of Cleveland, asked the people of the diocese to participate in a survey as one part of the diocesan listening process. In a later pastoral letter he reported that the most important issue for people was "homilies that relate to daily living." He interpreted this response by concluding, "That survey demonstrated unambiguously that we are a people of the word."[6]

Outstanding preachers develop the habit of looking at all of life through the lens of the scriptures interpreted in the light of daily experience. It is especially helpful for them to read next Sunday's scriptures early in the week so that news stories, films, television programs, radio talk shows and conversations with friends can provide insights about how the readings speak to real life. If the readings are held in mind as the week progresses, it is more likely that preachers will notice how often everyday life experiences will speak to God's word, and vice versa.

F. Is Engaging

Homilies that speak to people's real life experiences are not necessarily engaging simply because the topic is relevant and important. It is not just what is said but how preachers say it that invites listeners to become absorbed in the preaching event. Edward Fischer writes, "How an observation is made can thrill you with insight or put you to sleep. Wonderful news burdened with jargon is polluted, but the same information presented with distinction may add something to life."[7]

Constructing homilies that are *inductive*, rather than deductive, is one of the surest ways to engage listeners. Inductive preaching begins with the particular, the immediate or the concrete instance and moves toward the general and universal. Skillful preachers who choose just the right particular occasion do not even need to be explicit about the conclusion. The congregation will arrive at the conclusion on its own. When Jesus preached about how the word of God grows in people's hearts, he began not with a broad generalization, but with: "Hear this! A sower went out to sow. And as he sowed, some seed fell on the path, and the birds came and ate it up" (Mark 4:3-4).

Outstanding homilies also engage the listeners when they are preached in an open, rather than closed, system. Closed-system homilies are those in which preachers maintain complete control of the homily and its message. Preachers provide the answers to questions they themselves have asked. They choose examples and illustrations only from their own world of experience. The congregation is left on the outside, watching preachers develop the message. Open-system preaching engages the listeners by inviting their active participation throughout the homily. In the open system, preachers pose questions that encourage listeners to ask themselves their own questions. The examples and illustrations such preachers use evoke the listeners' experiences. The homily at the end of this chapter is an example of open-system preaching.

G. Has One Central Idea

Chapter Three, which deals with creating homilies, describes in detail how a homily develops one central idea rather than multiple ideas. At this point, it may be helpful to mention that outstanding homilies are more likely to engage the listeners throughout the entire message if they involve one simple, clear central idea. If preachers pack a homily with complex, multiple ideas, it is likely that the congregation will take away only part of the word.

H. Is Clear and Simple

Outstanding homilies are clear and simple. One preacher reported that the finest compliment he ever received in this regard was from a ten-year-old girl who told him, "Father, I always understand you when you preach." Simplicity in homilies does not mean talking down to a congregation, nor does it require stripping homilies of all distinction in order to appeal to the lowest common denominator. True simplicity in preaching never resorts to the hackneyed and unoriginal.

It may sound impressive to say, "In the locus of where may be found that which you tend to appraise more highly than any other possessions, there will be discerned your uttermost affective yearnings." It communicates more clearly to say, "For where your treasure is, there also will your heart be" (Luke 12:34). Although understanding and interpreting the scriptures require extensive scholarship, God's word as literature is amazingly simple in style. Outstanding homilies strive to reflect the style of the scriptures, which in many places proclaim a fathomless God in very simple human language. Edward Fischer observes, "In worship, too, the motto might well be: not too much rigmarole."[8]

When professional writers give advice to aspiring authors, many suggest that students read, read, read. Preachers who need to develop a simpler style would be wise to read the newspaper for examples of telling a story as simply as possible. Journalists know that the opening paragraph of a story must contain all the facts. Their readers should never have to dig through an entire story only to discover important details buried near the end. Homilies, of course, do not simply report facts, but the simplicity required of a journalist can be a valuable teaching tool for honing the skill of preaching with simplicity. Even so, the language of preaching and worship shares more with poetry than with journalism.

2. Homily Moves and Structures

How do preachers write homilies that stand apart from the ordinary? One of the most fundamental and important things to realize is that homilies are not written documents, but oral-aural events. Outstanding preaching is written to be spoken and heard.

Homilies exist only while they are actually spoken and heard at the liturgy. The written homily text is a plan for what preachers will say or a record of what has been preached. It is not the homily itself. Consequently, preachers should think of a homily as a series of oral *moves*, rather than a construction of homily points, or propositions. In *Homiletic Moves and Structures*, David Buttrick explores the notion of the homily as an oral-aural event. Good homilies, called sermons in his tradition, are not constructed as syllogisms that move from carefully argued premises to a conclusion. Articles intended for private reading can be crafted in complex language structures, but preaching poses a different challenge. In preaching as an oral-aural event, preachers and congregation progress through a series of language moves.

What Are Homily Moves?

> Sermons are a movement of language from one idea to
> another, each idea being shaped in a bundle of words.
> Thus, when we preach we speak in formed modules of
> language arranged in some patterned sequence. These
> modules of language we will call "moves."[9]

Buttrick's basic insight about constructing homilies as a series of
language moves can help those preachers who are accustomed to
writing homilies as if they were essays more suitable for private
reading. A written text intended for private reading can afford to be
complex in structure. Readers can return to a section of text if they
need to reexamine the thought. Spoken language exists just for the
moment. Preachers who are sensitive to the oral-aural nature of the
homily will strive to write in language modules that speak to the
ear.

Each homily move develops one image or idea in a clear style
that helps the hearer reach closure on that section of the homily
before being asked to proceed with the preacher to the next move:
"Every move has a shape, an internal design. The shape of a move
is determined in an interaction of (1) theological understanding, (2)
an eye for oppositions, and (3) actualities of lived experience."[10]

It is no revelation that well-written homily moves are informed
by sound theology and the lived experience of the congregation
and preacher. But what does Buttrick mean by maintaining "an eye
for oppositions"?

Certain homily moves, or elements within the moves, may cause
opposition in some listeners. If a homily proclaims that God loves
us unconditionally, for example, some listeners may ask themselves
whether their prayers and good works are meaningless, since God
puts no conditions on love. It is important that preachers anticipate
opposition and construct moves that clearly communicate a
response. Some communication theorists call this strategy "inocu-
lation."

Homily Moves and Rhetorical Intentions

Eucharistic homilies, preached in the context of worship, do not ordinarily announce God to unbelievers. They proclaim God already at work in the lives of believers: "Basic Christian rhetoric, then, involves 'bringing out,' 'associating,' and 'disassociating.' Moves in a sermon will develop from these basic rhetorical intentions."[11]

Homily moves help believers to name their faith experiences by bringing out the Lord's activity in their lives. In some instances, this naming is done by associating people and events from daily life with the mighty events proclaimed in the scriptures. Family members grieving at the funeral of a loved one can find consolation when their hurt is associated with Jesus weeping at the tomb of his friend Lazarus. At other times, homily moves involve disassociating experiences from God's activity. Countercultural preaching is one of the most common types of disassociation.

Example of Moves in Scripture

The Lectionary selections for each Eucharist can also be thought of in terms of moves. Looked at from this perspective, the readings appear as a series of interactions between God and people, rather than lessons with a point to be explained. Consider, for example, the account of Jesus' birth:

> In those days a decree went out from Caesar Augustus that the whole world should be enrolled. This was the first enrollment, when Quirinius was governor of Syria. So all went to be enrolled, each to his own town. And Joseph too went up from Galilee from the town of Nazareth to Judea, to the city of David that is called Bethlehem, because he was of the house and family of David, to be enrolled with Mary, his betrothed, who was with child. While they were there, the time came for her to have her child, and she gave birth to her firstborn son. She wrapped him in swaddling clothes and laid him in a manger, because there was no room for them in the inn. Now there were shepherds in that region living in the fields and keeping the night watch over their flock. The angel of the Lord appeared to them and the glory of the Lord shone around them, and they were struck with great fear. The angel said to them, "Do not be afraid; for behold, I proclaim to you good news of great joy that will

be for all the people. For today in the city of David a savior has been born for you who is Christ and Lord. And
this will be a sign for you: you will find an infant
wrapped in swaddling clothes and lying in a manger."
And suddenly there was a multitude of the heavenly host
with the angel, praising God and saying:
    "Glory to God in the highest
    and on earth peace to those on whom
        his favor rests."
When the angels went away from them to heaven, the
shepherds said to one another, "Let us go, then, to Bethlehem to see this thing that has taken place, which the
Lord has made known to us." So they went in haste and
found Mary and Joseph, and the infant lying in the
manger. When they saw this, they made known the message that had been told them about this child. All who
heard it were amazed by what had been told them by the
shepherds. And Mary kept all these things, reflecting on
them in her heart. Then the shepherds returned, glorifying and praising God for all they had heard and seen, just
as it had been told to them.

                                        Luke 2:1-20

The boxes on the next page demonstrate how this reading is
expressed as a series of moves, or language modules, instead of
points that explain something. Determining certain moves involves
some degree of arbitrary decision.

1. Caesar orders a census leading to a great pilgrimage to hometowns.	2. Joseph and his pregnant wife, Mary, travel to Bethlehem.	3. Mary gives birth to a boy whose crib is a manger.
4. An angel appears and the glory of God shines in the night.	5. The angel announces the birth of Jesus to shepherds.	6. A multitude of angels next appears praising God.
7. The angels return to heaven.	8. The shepherds decide to go see this great wonder.	9. The shepherds find the holy family just as promised.
10. People are astonished at hearing the shepherds' story.	11. Mary treasures all these events in her heart.	12. The shepherds return, glorifying God for what they heard and saw.

Preaching the Moves

When preachers examine this story of Luke's gospel as a series of moves, the story takes on a new dimension. It is no longer just an account *about* the birth of Jesus. The story appears more as a series of actions, of God's moves in human history. Preachers may note that any particular move would be an especially appropriate place to focus the homily, considering their own congregation. A homily need not begin by talking about the first move in the scripture text, nor does one homily have to preach about every move.

The following homily illustrates the way one preacher centered on the scripture's moves that deal with angels, glory and shepherds. The preacher chose to focus only on these moves because of the particular occasion and congregation: The homily was prepared for Christmas Midnight Mass at a parish in Las Vegas, Nevada, a desert city that has its own experience of light. In this sample homily, the phrase in brackets at the start of each section names each move and provides clues to the development of the homily.

3. Sample Homily: Christmas

[Las Vegas and Unfulfilled Promises] Christmas night is a time of promises. The shepherds heard some marvelous promises this night. People throughout the world are celebrating this night in small rural churches and large city cathedrals, hearing the old story of God's promises. You and I celebrate in a very unique city. Las Vegas makes promises too. This city exists on its promise of fun, excitement, riches and happiness. The Chamber of Commerce may not like to hear it, but our city cannot fulfill its promise to make us truly happy. No city, no earthly power for that matter, can make us truly happy in the sense of fulfilling the reason we were created. The gospel for this Christmas night tells us why that is. This story takes place in another desert area. If we were to drive out beyond the bright lights of Las Vegas this chilly night, the countryside might look and feel very much like Bethlehem, the desert town where this story takes place.

[Ancient Promises] The real story does not start with the Bethlehem of the first Christmas night. We must go back many hundreds of years earlier to find the shepherd boy David tending his flocks. Scripture tells us young David was a handsome youth, but shepherds were certainly not among the beautiful people. In fact, shepherds of this time were among the most "undesirable" types. You would not want a shepherd as a houseguest. God took this shepherd and made him king over God's own people. God worked powerful wonders through David and granted great military victories through him. God had much more than that in David's future. God promised that a mighty savior would one day be born in David's line. And the people waited. And they waited.

[Waiting for Promises to Be Fulfilled] Children know what it is like waiting for promises to be fulfilled, especially waiting for Christmas. When I was a little boy, my mother used to promise me, "Christmas is just around the corner—be patient!" It was hard to wait. God's people waited for something far more important than Christmas gifts. They had heard the great ancient promises that a messiah would be sent to them from God. They had no idea who this person would be, only that the savior would be powerful and would lead them as God's own special people. That was the promise, and they waited. Do you wait and long for something you want very much? This desert night, Mary and Joseph too waited for a savior as they journeyed to Bethlehem. They longed for a savior.

[Something About to Happen] At last the long wait is about to end. We hear in this gospel the solemn announcement, "In those days a decree went out from Caesar Augustus...." This is a big deal. Caesar Augustus was famous for bringing the peace of the Roman Empire to many nations, including this desert people. Caesar Augustus had a coin minted showing the temple of war with the doors closed—he closed those doors, the coin says. Caesar Augustus brought peace. But not real peace. Caesar could bring only the absence of military conflict. The one who alone can bring genuine peace is about to burst into this night.

[Angelic Floorshow] And then it happens. The angels split the desert night wide open with an array of light and singing and proclamations in a performance that not even Las Vegas could match. You and I can walk down the strip and see a volcano erupt every night at the Mirage Hotel. We can see a pirate battle at Treasure Island, but those shows pale in comparison to this one in the desert near Bethlehem. The angels electrify the desert night at Bethlehem. And who is the audience for this heavenly spectacle? Mangy shepherds. Shepherds like David was once. This is God's way of saying that the promises made to the shepherd David long ago are now fulfilled. The message from the angels is, "Glory to God in the highest—this day a savior is born in David's city." The longing and the waiting are over. It is all happening now!

[True Peace of Jesus Is for Now] A key message of the angel is that all of the wonder happens "this day." The angel meant, of course, that momentous day in history when God became one of us. Their words about so much joy happening "this day" also mean this day in our own time. We are not just looking back at a moment in the past. The Lord continues to break into our lives here and now. Jesus offers to us, this day, the kind of peace that no one or no thing can offer. Have we been looking for lasting peace in the wrong places? Have we thought we would have real peace if we just had a bit more money? Or perhaps we have fallen for the promise of television commercials that suggests if we just have the right car or the right body or even the right bowl of cornflakes we will be really happy. Those things might offer brief moments of happiness and even hints of peace, but not the true peace that Jesus offers this day.

[True Peace and Continual Struggle] There is a bittersweet message in the angels' voices this day. They shout out joyfully that Jesus' birth brings "glory to God and peace on earth." Those same words will be heard much later in the gospel, but with a note of sadness. We know the infant Jesus will grow up to be a man, will suffer and die for the forgiveness of our sins. Near the end of Jesus' life when he enters Jerusalem, the crowds will yell out, "Blessed is he who comes as king in the name of the Lord! Peace in heaven and glory in the highest!" The bittersweet message this day is that life and death usually go hand in hand in our human experience. Jesus knew that, and he was willing to embrace it. And so also this day Jesus asks that we embrace that mystery. Despite the joy of this day, we will continue to face difficulties. Amid the joy some experience of visiting with distant family these holidays, they know they will soon have to leave. Some in our midst face trials and crosses that we might not want to think about on this joyful day. That is all part of the good news of this day. Although Jesus calls us to bear the cross with him, this day he promises final victory. The peace brought by Caesar Augustus ended long ago.

The Roman Empire is long gone. However, the peace and the victory that Jesus brings are here today, and they are lasting. Nothing can defeat the power of this day. This day there is born for us a savior who has fulfilled all that has been promised. And the peace he brings cannot be defeated. Ultimately there is victory because of this day.

[Mary Treasured All These Things] There is one final detail about the events on this desert morning. After the shepherds finally see Jesus in the manger, they rush off to tell others what they have seen. We hear that the listeners are "astonished." That does not mean they actually believed. Mary was different. She treasured all these wonders and pondered them in her heart. Mary shows that we believers let this message of Jesus take hold in our hearts and minds so that we are truly changed. When we go forth from this church tonight, let us walk with the same kind of joy that the shepherds had. Wouldn't it be great if people on the Las Vegas strip saw our faces this night and wondered, "Why are they so happy?" Wouldn't it be amazing if we told them all we had seen and heard tonight? May we give to all we meet something to ponder and treasure in their hearts.

Further Reading

LaCugna, Catherine Mowry. "Reflections on Preaching the Word of God." *America*, 19 March 1994, 4-5.

Pilla, Anthony. "Ministry of the Word." *Origins* 25 (1995): 277-87.

Notes

1. John Paul Heil, *The Gospel of Mark as a Model for Action* (New York: Paulist Press, 1992).

2. Robert Maloney, Lent Letter to Members of the Congregation of the Mission, 1993.

3. Walter J. Burghardt, "From Study to Proclamation," in *A New Look At Preaching*, ed. John Burke (Wilmington, Del.: Michael Glazier, 1983), p. 34.

4. Walter Burghardt, address, Aquinas Great Preacher of the Year Award, St. Louis, 28 April 1995.

5. Henry Nouwen, *Creative Ministry* (Garden City, N.Y.: Doubleday, 1971), p. 35.

6. Anthony Pilla, "The Ministry of the Word," *Origins* 25 (1995): 279.

7. Edward Fischer, *Everybody Steals from God* (Notre Dame, Ind.: University of Notre Dame Press, 1977), pp. 33-34.

8. Fischer, p. 111.

9. David Buttrick, *Homiletic Moves and Structures* (Philadelphia: Fortress, 1987), p. 23.

10. Buttrick, p. 33.

11. Buttrick, p. 42.

Chapter Three

Creating a Homily

Telling the Old Story in a Fresh Way

In a homiletics class, I asked seminarians to write a paper on the identity of a preacher in light of their reading and class discussions. Most of the students wrote well-crafted, organized explanations anchored in solid theological and theoretical foundations. One student submitted "The Diver."[1] In this poem, he connects the experience of a preacher beginning a homily with the experience of a diver about to leap from a towering cliff into the water.

The Diver	**The Preacher**
A diver	A preacher
climbs the summit peak	assumes the pulpit
bathed in scarlet light.	steeped in the Word of God.
A diver	A preacher
somewhere between heaven	somewhere between God
and the sea.	and man.
Eyes lifted and arms poised,	Eyes raised in prayer and arms in
he takes in the sky's reds,	blessing,
which fade into orange	he drinks deeply of the Lord,
and melt into yellow streaks.	who fades into the Word
He looks down to the sea	and melts into words.
and gazes into the same fiery red	He surveys the congregation
dancing on the water.	and gazes into the reflection of
He will join the sea but	God
not the fiery red blaze he	in the faces of his Church.
now perceives, but a cool	He will join the ranks of men but
dark destiny	not the image of his God he
lulled by hidden torrents and	now perceives, but a broken
currents.	chained rank
He stands for a second,	lulled by hidden temptations and
gathering his thoughts	pains.

The Diver (cont.)

in concentration for his dive,
ready to split eternity into
eternity past and eternity future,
and he contemplates his own
 significance.
Sky or sea?
He leaps.
He comes to life in the span.
For a second he is brother to
 the wind.
Held only by the sky ablaze
free of land and sea.
He is kin to the sun that chooses
its own path.
He knows not weight nor
 boundaries.
Brother to the wind, kin to
 the sun,
he knows complete freedom.
He soars, rapt in flight. Only
then he penetrates the sea,
breaking the perfect mirror of
 the sky.
He slips into the water depth.
He plunges the depths, knows
 darkness.
The water gives way and breaks
 his fall.
It buoys him up, slowing his
 movement.
His place is between the torch fire
 of the heavens
and the dark depth of the sea.
Both meet in him.

The Preacher (cont.)

He stands for a second,
gathering his thoughts
in concentration for his message,
ready to split eternity into
eternity past and eternity future,
and he contemplates his own
 significance.
God's Word or man's?
He speaks.
He comes to life in the span.
For a second he is brother to the
 Spirit.
Held only by God's promise
free of man and sin.
He is kin to God who chooses
his own path.
He knows not chains nor death.
Brother to the Spirit, kin to God,
he knows complete freedom.
He speaks, rapt in prayer. Only
then he penetrates his charges,
breaking the perfect mirror of
 God's glory.
He slips into his humble rank.
He plunges the depth, knows
 darkness.
The hearts give way and break his
 fall.
The congregation buoys him up,
slowing his temptation.
His place is between the glory of
 God
and the dark weakness of men.
Both meet in him.

Most of the students in the class wrote typical theological trea-
tises that described the preacher's identity in traditional language.
They were content that they were fulfilling the assignment. One
very creative student chose to express his theoretical understanding
in a poem. His work offers an unusual insight into the preacher's
self-understanding. The use of a poem suggests that the weekly task
of crafting God's word in human language is enlivened when it is
allowed to be a creative process. Some ministers confess that homily preparation is the most difficult part of their week. A common
complaint goes: "I have said all I have to say about these readings.
There is simply nothing new that I can tell my people." Preachers
who have given homilies on the same scriptures to the same congregation probably do not have anything new to say. Preaching is
not about conveying new information, but about proclaiming an
old story in a fresh way. Preaching is not concerned with increasing
the listener's store of information, but with the believer's transformation. The creative process is in the ability to clothe the word
with fresh insight and craft the message in unique forms.

This chapter deals with three areas involved in writing homilies.
The first explores imagination and the creative process. The second
describes five fundamental questions preachers need to ask, whatever the preparation method they use. The chapter concludes with
a description of one method many preachers have found helpful in
the creative process of writing fresh homilies that preach the old
story Sunday after Sunday.

1. The Creative Process

Creativity resists systematic analysis and constricting rules. It
usually dwells in the unconscious level where it is difficult to
observe and categorize. "The Diver" was a creative way for one student to describe how it feels to plunge into the preaching process.
How did the author arrive at the poem? Why did he think of a cliff
diver as he reflected on the identity of the preacher? What is the
creative process?

Creativity and Relationships

Creative people have the imagination to see relationships among
seemingly unrelated events, ideas, persons and other elements of

their experience. "Imagination makes correlations happen."[2] Jesus held a few tiny mustard seeds in his hand and preached about how faith gradually grows in the hearts of believers. He knew that a bit of yeast mixed into dough eventually causes the entire mass to rise. This experience enriched his preaching about the way believers are to act as leaven as they spread faith throughout a community. The seminarian who wrote "The Diver" had the vision to see that preachers who climb into the pulpit, like cliff divers who plunge into the water below, take a risk in plunging into their ministry. People with this kind of vision have a gift for describing complex and elusive realities in terms of the simple and familiar. They have found ways to make connections that allow others to share their insights. Creative people can imagine.

Research on cognitive processes shows how the left and right hemispheres of the brain have unique functions in communication. Left-brain thinking is linear, dealing with information in logical, organized patterns. The left brain perceives reality according to the way events occur in time, one step after another. The right brain is more intuitive than logical. It processes the whole picture at one time. Right-brain thinking is impressionistic, organizing reality in space rather than time.[3] The specific functions of each hemisphere have consequences for preaching. Preachers use both hemispheres in shaping balanced homilies. Left-brain functions help preachers explain complex ideas in clear, precise speech. Right-brain functions allow preachers to use images. If homilies are to speak to the whole person, not just the logical, linear consciousness, preachers need to discover imaginative connections that allow people to experience the word and also understand the word.

The Risk of Imagination

Imagination is suspect in some academic settings. As students, we were taught to think logically, carefully weighing cause and effect. Teachers encouraged us to be suspicious of what cannot be demonstrated. It is all the better if things can be proven, the thinking went. That type of left-brain process plays a crucial role in education. Unfortunately, some believe it is the only valid way to learn. The right-brain power of imagination sees beyond the reality of the way things are, and allows one to see the way things could be. An image has the power to evoke the unique experience of the listener. "While thinking may distance us from reality, imagination allows us to experience a person or thing in its uniqueness, engaging the ordinary and the particular of life."[4]

Imaginative preachers risk giving up control of the message, because imagination allows listeners to take a message into their own hands. Images do not limit thinking. Images, rather, open a whole realm of responses unique to each listener. Preachers who simply explain the faith through linear arguments can do no more than impose conclusions on the congregation. But preachers who employ images evoke the personal faith experiences through which God is at work in people's lives.[5] The following homily segments illustrate how a linear argument directs a particular response, while an image evokes many different responses.

Example: Linear Preaching

Today is the Feast of the Holy Family of Jesus, Mary and Joseph. This feast reminds us of the sanctity of marriage and family life. Today, the family is under attack. Divorce, abortion, spousal and child abuse threaten the family. As Christians, we must have the courage to stand firm for authentic family values.

The catechism reminds us that children owe *filial piety* to their parents. Parents have the duty of providing sound education and moral formation for their children. You who are children must heed the words of Proverbs that counsel you to "keep your father's commandment, and forsake not your mother's teaching." While children continue to live in the home they must respect their parents. Even as they mature and leave home they should still show respect. Parents bear the important responsibility of providing a good home environment for their children. Parents are the first Christian evangelizers of their children. This is not an obligation to be taken lightly.

Example: Image Preaching

James McBride is a black man who is very proud of his white mother, Ruth McBride Jordan. In *The Color of Water*, he describes how she raised him and his eleven brothers and sisters. Despite the financial problems that go with having such a large family, his mother was determined to provide a good education for all of her children. She successfully sought grants and scholarships to send all twelve children to college. Ruth McBride Jordan is a woman of strength who believes in family.

This feast of the Holy Family is an earthy reminder that Jesus was a real human with parents, a hometown, chores around the house, hopes and disappointments. The scriptures say little about Jesus' family life. You and I know about families. Some of us may have come from happy families that rival the joy of the Holy Family. Some here may have grown up in broken homes or been raised by people other than their birth parents. Our own experience of family life teaches us something important about Jesus. He understands that it sometimes takes strength to live as a family. Jesus, like Ruth McBride Jordan, believes in family.

The example written in a linear style explains what children and parents are obliged to do as members of a Christian family. The preacher possesses the information and clearly sets the teaching before the congregation. The second example evokes the experience of family unique to each listener. The story of how Ruth McBride Jordan worked to provide education for twelve children allows both parents and children to connect with their own experiences of the sacrifices involved in family life. Images do not constrict the listener to arrive at one conclusion. They evoke as many responses as there are listeners. The example of image preaching also invites the listener to realize that Jesus understands them as members who strive to live as family, despite the kind of family they know.

Functions of Imagination

Imagination in preaching allows listeners to enter the homily on the level of their own faith experience. Paul Scott Wilson refines this dynamic further by describing three functions of imagination: prophetic, ethical and poetic.[6]

Prophetic Imagination

This kind of imagination "discerns the discrepancy between God's intentions for the world, as revealed in scripture, and the world as it actually is."[7] Preachers with prophetic imagination are not content with the way things are. They set before the believers a vision of how things can be. Walter Brueggemann describes this prophetic vision in terms of an alternative consciousness that has the twofold function of "dismantling the dominant consciousness" as it "serves to *energize* persons and communities by its promise of another time and situation toward which the community of faith may move."[8]

The previous chapter described how outstanding preaching is not content with simply describing the ills of society. It is relatively easy to be concrete and specific in talking about sinful situations. Outstanding preaching presents an equally concrete image of what believers can do and be. Preachers with prophetic imagination offer stories of persons and events that enflesh the promise of what the world can be when Christ is allowed to be fully alive in the believer.

Ethical Imagination

As an expression of the second function of imagination in preaching, Wilson cites Jesus' great commandment that we love God and our neighbor. Imagination can invite believers to empathize with the struggles of others by seeing them as persons possessing the dignity of God's children. "Ethical imagination in preaching points to ethical boundaries or the results of those boundaries having been crossed. It is at the same time compassionate expression with wide-open spaces of salvation...."[9]

Preaching characterized by ethical imagination does not merely espouse moralistic platitudes. It takes little creativity or imagination to tell a congregation that "God expects us all to be merciful to others." Jesus placed a lively merciful image before his people in telling them about the king who forgave one of his subjects a great debt. When that subject met a fellow servant who owed him a small sum, he began to beat him, demanding that he repay the small debt (Matthew 18:23-35). This powerful image invites a listener to see the face of greed in the wicked servant and hear the harsh voice of one who will not forgive as he was forgiven.

Poetic Imagination

The third function of imagination in preaching is poetic, or interpretive. This is the area of imagination dealing in metaphors, similes and other figures of speech that connect two previously unconnected ideas in a way that produces new meaning.[10] "The Diver" linked two seemingly unrelated ideas to offer new insights into the self-understanding of a preacher leaping into ministry. Karl Rahner speaks of the poet as one who is best able to get through to the hearts of listeners. When the poet is also priest, able to see God's grace at work in all of creation, "[t]hen it is grace. It proclaims that *everything* is redeemed. The primordial words of man, transmuted by the Spirit of God, are allowed to become words of God, because a poet has become a priest."[11]

Habits of Creative Persons

There are techniques that help develop creativity and imagination. A good starting point involves observing how creative people work. Brewster Ghiselin does this in *The Creative Process*.[12] He examines various works of Einstein, van Gogh, Wordsworth, Henry James and other great artists and intellectuals, concluding that nearly all creative people describe several common experiences, some of which are explained here.

Preverbal Hunch

"Creation begins typically with a vague, even a confused excitement, some sort of yearning, hunch, or other preverbal intimation of approaching or potential resolution."[13] In the earliest stages of creating a homily, preachers may not be able to verbalize themes or theses within the scriptural texts. This is partly because the word is not about some*thing* as much as it is the story of some*one*. When preachers as believers experience God in the word, that experience may resist verbal constraints in the first stages of homily preparation.

Dissatisfaction with the Ordinary and Familiar

Creative people are not satisfied with the old way of doing things. "The first need is therefore to transcend the old order."[14] Creative preachers are not content with a hastily abstracted theme from one or more of the Lectionary readings. They do not wish to let others experience the word *for them*, but need to allow the word of God to be filtered through their own faith lives. Once they begin to write, creative preachers will not settle for a standard three-point development. They seek lively, fresh ways of telling the old story so that it may be heard in fresh ways.

Unclear Solution

The initial vague hunch or preverbal experience of the word is enough to set preachers off on their investigation without needing to know the end of the process. "It is essential to remember that the creative end is never in full sight at the beginning and that it is brought wholly into view only when the process of creation is completed."[15]

Gestation

The creative process cannot be rushed. Nearly all creative people counsel patience while ideas and images are allowed time to gestate.[16] Preachers cannot expect creative, fresh homilies to emerge if they attempt to write them the night before they are to be preached.

Creative Strategies

Openness to All of Life

Ghiselin's study shows that creative people live creative lives. They do not turn creativity on and off whenever it is time to settle down to work. Walter Burghardt's lifelong experience as a preacher has taught him the importance of always being open to homiletic insights: "From anthropology to zoology, whatever you learn about God's creation is potential grist for your homiletic mill."[17] Anne Lamott echoes this sentiment in her instructions for creative writing. She tells students to develop the children's sense of wonder that causes them to look at all of life as a sacrament of God's love and presence. The child can look at a tree, a building or a flower and say, "Wow!" We adults tend to get wrapped up in ourselves to the extent that we take all these small wonders for granted. In her sometimes indelicate style, Lamott urges aspiring writers to pull their heads out from the place where they have been stuck so they can look around and offer a bit of hope to the world.[18] Her advice is apropos for preachers who are sometimes too preoccupied with church affairs to realize that their people are living in a much wider world. Along with this general attitude of being open to all of life, there are specific strategies preachers can use to develop creativity and imagination.

Note Cards

Many writers have the habit of jotting down notes when they have an idea that might be used in a later work. Anne Lamott always carries index cards and a pen with her. As a writer she constantly observes life, whether she is walking alone in the woods or standing in the supermarket checkout line. If she overhears a conversation or has any type of insight she jots it down. She acknowledges that this may not be the best method for everyone. Some writers have the type of memory that allows them to make mental notes of important observations.[19] PDAs (Personal Digital Assistants) provide very convenient ways for preachers to take notes when observations on life might otherwise be lost.

Tape Recorders

Small dictation tape recorders offer an alternative to carrying note cards and pens and PDAs. Preachers may find themselves to be more expressive if they record their impressions of an experience as it happens. For these individuals, written notes can be too brief and cryptic. One preacher has the habit of carrying a small recorder in his car. As he drives to hospital visits, communion calls and meetings, the recorder is handy for noting any insights that may strike him. Since he reads the following Sunday's Lectionary selections early in the week, he feels more attuned to people, events and experiences that enflesh abstract homily ideas.

Creativity Exercises

If preachers are able to work in groups, as described in the appendix, they may wish to try exercises that are designed to develop creativity and imagination. The Academy of Homiletics, an ecumenical organization of homiletics teachers, commissioned a study on new ways to foster the desire to learn to preach. Their results suggest several strategies for developing creativity: "mini-dramas, shared journal entries, exercises in interpretive movement, free association with biblical images, and creative responses to literary and cinematic arts...."[20]

At one parish's recent Holy Thursday Eucharist, the pastor offered an example of how a mini-drama can enhance a homily. As the deacon read the account of the Last Supper (John 13:1-15), the pastor silently acted out the movements of Jesus. When the deacon read that Jesus "rose from supper and took off his outer garments," the pastor stood and removed his chasuble. The priest tied a towel around his waste, poured water in a basin, and washed the feet of those to be baptized at the Saturday vigil, as these parts of the gospel were read. At the conclusion of the foot washing, the pastor continued the gospel from memory as he addressed those soon to be baptized. As he began, "Do you realize what I have done for you?" there was a profound sense of being at the Last Supper. The section of the appendix that relates to this chapter offers several exercises on creativity.

2. Five Fundamental Questions

For centuries, people have watched apples fall to the earth without asking why. Not until the seventeenth century, at least according to legend, did Isaac Newton ask, "Why does the apple fall to earth?" Only by asking the right question was the great mathematician and physicist able to formulate the law of gravity. *There is tremendous power in asking the right questions.* It is the same in crafting a fresh homily. The process begins not by looking for facile themes or glib answers, but when preachers ask the right questions. This section deals with five fundamental questions for preachers to ask in preparing homilies. These questions of themselves do not constitute a complete homily preparation process. They are the fundamental questions preachers must ask themselves, regardless of the method they use to prepare homilies. Unless the preacher has asked each of the fundamental questions, the homily will be missing a crucial element. By way of example, each of these fundamental questions is posed in light of a familiar scripture text, the story of the Samaritan.

There was a scholar of the law who stood up to test Jesus and said, "Teacher, what must I do to inherit eternal life?" Jesus said to him, "What is written in the law? How do you read it?" He said in reply, "You shall love the Lord, your God, with all your heart, with all your being, with all your strength, and with all your mind, and your neighbor as yourself." He replied to him, "You have answered correctly; do this and you will live."

But because he wished to justify himself, he said to Jesus, "And who is my neighbor?" Jesus replied, "A man fell victim to robbers as he went down from Jerusalem to Jericho. They stripped and beat him and went off leaving him half-dead. A priest happened to be going down that road, but when he saw him, he passed by on the opposite side. Likewise a Levite came to the place, and when he saw him, he passed by on the opposite side. But a Samaritan traveler who came upon him was moved with compassion at the sight. He approached the victim, poured oil and wine over his wounds and bandaged them. Then he lifted him up on his own animal, took him to an inn, and cared for him. The next day he took out two silver coins and gave them to the innkeeper with the instruction, 'Take care of him. If you spend more than what I have given you, I shall repay you on my way back.' Which of these three, in your opinion, was neighbor to the robbers' victim?" He answered, "The one who treated him with mercy." Jesus said to him, "Go and do likewise."

Luke 10:25-37

A. What Is the Scripture Saying?

The first of the fundamental questions asks, "What is the scripture saying?" Another way of asking this question might be, "What do I believe about this text?" The question is not, "What will I say about each of the readings this Sunday?" because preachers begin their homily preparation by listening to the scriptures rather than by deciding what topic they wish to develop.

If preachers begin preparing a homily by deciding what they will say about this gospel of the Samaritan, they may too readily jump to the conclusion that the homily should talk about the need to be charitable to one's neighbor. This would be an obvious starting point, especially considering the context of the Samaritan story. The account directly follows the two great commandments and precedes Jesus' admonition, "Go and do likewise." Preachers may reach a different conclusion if they start by asking, "What is the scripture saying?" rather than "What will the homily be about?"

Douglas Oakman asks what the Samaritan story is saying by looking through the lens of a social-science critic sensitive to how the original audience would have heard Jesus' story, according to their own world view.[21] He notes that the final verse that asks which of the characters was a true neighbor was not part of Luke's original material. That verse makes the account of the Samaritan a mere example story. If that verse is omitted, however, the listener has to ask what the story is saying as it stands on its own. Oakman's basic insight is that Jesus was a peasant telling a story to other peasants. The storyteller and many listeners were in sympathy with the beaten man, but they were suspicious of the Samaritan. He was not one of them. The Samaritan was both a Gentile and a wealthy merchant with oil and wine to sell, and a beast to haul his inventory. He should have stayed among his own people. Furthermore, inns of that time were incredibly unsavory places, and innkeepers were not to be trusted. In giving the innkeeper a blank check, the Samaritan was risking the possibility that the unscrupulous innkeeper would hold the injured man hostage in order to make more money.

These details suggest that, as in other parables, this is a story that shows what the kingdom is like. God, reflected in the Samaritan, is a generous giver, even to the point of indebting himself for whatever is required. It also tells us where the kingdom is found: in the most unexpected and unsavory places. The kingdom also turns our world upside down, challenging and transforming society. Oakman's exegesis turns the focus of the story away from what we should do as good Christians and allows the story to tell us who God is and what the kingdom is like.

B. What Is the Central Idea?

The second fundamental question asks, "What is the central idea of the homily?" A well-crafted homily develops one idea, not multiple ideas. If preachers cannot summarize the heart of the homily in one simple sentence, they most likely have more than one homily on their hands. In consideration of the exegesis, one central idea for the homily might be, "God goes overboard in doing what is necessary to draw us into the kingdom." This central idea establishes the focus for the homily in that it directs the preacher to preach the God of the kingdom, rather than what we people need to be doing.

A poor central idea would be, "We must not be like the priest and Levite in this story who passed by their neighbor in need. We also need to avoid prejudice, like those listening to Jesus who may be shocked that a foreigner turned out to be the hero. Like God, imaged in the Samaritan, we should go out of our way in generosity." This statement, which requires three sentences, will lead to at least three different homilies. Central ideas are expressed in one simple sentence that gives precise focus to the message.

C. What Is the Preacher's Experience?

The third fundamental question is, "How have I personally experienced the central idea of this homily?" In asking this question, preachers go beyond what they *know* about the central idea, and even beyond what they *believe* about the central idea. They are asking how they themselves, in their own faith journey, have experienced (or not experienced) this word of God. People in the pews are not especially interested in what preachers can articulate in highly polished lectures. They are vitally interested in what preachers have experienced in their personal relationship with the Lord. Pope Paul VI observed, "Modern man listens more willingly to witnesses than to teachers, and if he does listen to teachers, it is because they are also witnesses."[22]

In light of Paul VI's observation, preachers are called to witness to their faith in the God of the Samaritan story more than they are called to explain the story. Presenting a talk *about* a generous God is not enough if preachers have gotten in touch with the God to whom they turn when they are in great need. Do they find a God willing to hand them a blank check as the Samaritan did with the innkeeper?

Although preachers question themselves about their personal experience of God's word, they do not need to share every explicit detail of their personal story with the congregation during the homily. Much of this experience is private. Talking about it could easily make preachers, and not God or God's word, the center of attention. When preachers reflect on these very private experiences, they get in touch with the God they know, not just the God they know *about.*

D. What Is the Listener's Experience?

Preachers next ask, "What is the *listener's* experience of the central idea?" Because homilies are about personal transformation more than they are about conveying information, preachers speak to the faith experience of the congregation, not just to their intellects. Effective preachers find creative ways to be in touch with the faith experience of the people to whom they preach. This is a detail often overlooked in preaching. Too much of the homily's content is from the preacher's world, and not enough from the listeners' world. Advertisers have full-time staffs with large budgets dedicated to finding out what people want, or at least what people would be willing to buy. Preachers do not need to find ways of packaging the gospel so it appeals to people. The gospel has its own power to attract. Preachers need to listen to the congregation to appreciate how they, the preachers, can proclaim a word that speaks to the congregation in their daily lives.

The Samaritan Story and the Congregation's Experience

What do people believe about the God they encounter in the story of the Samaritan? Is this the God believers experience in their day-to-day faith lives? Is God someone who writes a blank check for them? Do they believe in a God who will do whatever it takes to show love for them? What does this God offer to a teenager addicted to drugs? Is this God good news for the single father or mother struggling to raise children by themselves? What does this God say to the elderly woman who sits alone all day in a nursing home wondering why family and friends do not visit? Theological abstractions will not fill these hungry hearts. Pious clichés are of little use to people who dare to ask if the God reflected in Samaritan story truly knows them and cares for them.

Homily Feedback Group

How do preachers get in touch with the faith lives of the congregation? One of the obvious ways is to listen carefully as people tell their personal stories. Preachers could ask a group of six or eight people to meet after Mass to talk about the homily. Preachers could pose several questions about how the message touched the listeners' daily lives. This can be an enlightening time, especially for preachers who tend to live too much in their own world. Whatever method preachers use to listen to their listeners, they do need to ask how the preached word touches people where they live. A later chapter discusses this important topic in greater detail.

E. What Is the Purpose of This Homily?

The last of the five fundamental questions asks, "What is the purpose of this particular homily?" "What would the preacher like to see happen in the lives of the listeners?" Another way to pose the question is, "Why is the preacher presenting this particular message and not another?" Preachers might even dare to ask themselves, "Here is the message—so what?" In whatever form preachers choose to frame the question, they are not asking what the homily is about, but what they hope the homily will achieve. Every homily has the same general purpose of bringing God's word into contact with God's people. Besides that general purpose, each homily also has a particular aim. Thirty years ago, my old homiletics teacher used to say, "Preaching is like shooting an arrow. If you aim at nothing, chances are very good that you will hit nothing." In asking themselves about the purpose of this homily, preachers are looking for specific responses in the lives of the listeners.

The Purpose of Preaching the Samaritan Story

A good central idea for a homily on the Samaritan story would proclaim the God who stops at nothing in loving people. Preachers still need to ask why they would want to preach this message. What would preachers hope people in the congregation might do because of hearing this homily? Perhaps they might hope that alienated Catholics would return to the sacrament of reconciliation in order to encounter this generous God in the sacrament. In this case, the homily might emphasize the Samaritan's generous blank check given to the innkeeper. This God stands in sharp contrast to some of the unpleasant experiences people may have had with a stern confessor. Consider a very different preaching situation where the homily is directed to young people who tend to be very exclusive about who belongs in their group and who is not welcomed. The homily might center on the people in Jesus' audience who thought the Samaritan should stay with his own kind. Whatever the particular preaching situation, when preachers ask themselves why they are preaching the homily, the message is likely to take a more specific, concrete direction.

The Homily Is Not Finished Yet

Once preachers have asked themselves these five fundamental questions, it does not mean that the homily is fully prepared. These questions comprise only the skeleton of the process. Preachers still need a preparation method that helps them form a well-crafted homily. Whatever method they choose, a crucial element of the homily will be missing, unless each of the five fundamental questions is asked and answered.

3. Moving from the Scriptures to the Finished Homily

The following method, which includes a dozen steps, is one way to deal with the sometimes daunting task of getting from the scriptures to the final homily. This method is particularly helpful for preachers who face writers' block. The process helps preachers begin preparing a homily without needing a clear sense of where the journey will eventually take them. Creative people often report that they start a work without being sure of its conclusion.

Anne Lamott teaches writers to approach the creative process "bird by bird." This title of her book comes from advice her father gave to her young brother who was facing the monumental task of writing a school report on birds that was due the next day. The boy had put off the assignment until the last moment. He was paralyzed by the task, until his father advised him, "Bird by bird, buddy. Just take it bird by bird."[23] Lamott counsels writers to divide the creative task into smaller, manageable pieces. The following method of preparing homilies channels creative energy by dividing the process into manageable steps. Five of these steps are identical to the five fundamental questions discussed in the previous section. The five questions, as already noted, belong in every preparation method.

A. Listen to the Scriptures

This step, the first of the five fundamental questions, is nearly always the starting point for preparing a liturgical homily, since the homily flows from the scriptures and leads into the rest of the Eucharistic liturgy. Any other starting point—an important upcoming parish event or a celebration such as Mother's Day—would likely lead preachers into preparing sermons rather than liturgical homilies.

B. Look for a General Theme

The first reading and the gospel have been chosen for the same Sunday in the Lectionary because they have parallel themes. Both readings may be linked by themes such as faith, repentance or God's love. These general themes are not central ideas. They serve only to point preachers in a certain direction.

C. Brainstorm

Group facilitators often encourage brainstorming as a way of generating new ideas. The process begins when the group is presented with a particular idea or issue that requires development. Group members then brainstorm by telling others about images, ideas, metaphors, personalities, items in the news or anything else that comes to mind concerning the given topic. It is important not to give negative feedback to anyone's comments. When group members feel free to say anything that comes to mind, no matter how potentially unhelpful, some very creative ideas often emerge. If preachers are preparing a homily alone, they can brainstorm by writing down as many images, quotes, connections with other scriptures, stories or anything else that comes to mind. If preparing in a group, someone can write down all the comments made by group members. Brainstorming is not the time to edit. All statements are created equal at this phase.

D. Narrow the Theme

The list generated in the brainstorming step will most likely have many images, quotes and ideas that cluster into several thematic groups. In this step, preacher look for clusters of items that suggest an initial direction for the homily. This is the time to eliminate all the unusable brainstorming items that emerged along with the helpful ones. Some items that do not fit may be used in another homily. As the list is narrowed, preachers will begin to focus the direction and purpose for the eventual homily. This is also a good place in the process to add further items to the list.

E. Phrase the Central Idea in One Simple Sentence

At this point, preachers formulate the central idea of the homily in one simple sentence that will focus the rest of the creative process. This central idea will become the standard by which the preacher or preachers decide what belongs and what does not belong in this particular homily.

F. What Is the Preacher's Experience of the Central Idea?

The discussion of the five fundamental questions in this chapter already stressed the importance of preachers needing to move beyond what they *think* about the message and reflect on their personal faith *experience* of the message.

G. What Is the Congregation's Experience of the Central Idea?

This is another of the fundamental questions discussed earlier. Later chapters on preaching the scriptures and listening to the listeners will continue to explore strategies for including other voices in the preacher's homily.

H. Determine the Homily's Purpose

In this step—another of the five fundamental questions—preachers take the central idea one step further by asking themselves why they are preaching this message. What do they hope will happen in the faith lives of the listeners as a result of this homily?

I. Outline the Homily Moves

Chapter Two described how homilies can be organized according to moves, or language modules. In outlining the message at this point in the process, preachers begin to gain a sense of how much time they wish to allot for each move. If an outline of the homily shows that the most important move occurs after three or four relatively unimportant moves, for example, preachers can allot less attention and time to these less important moves. This frees more time for those moves in the homily that proclaim the central idea.

Preachers who begin writing without an outline risk giving too much emphasis to homily moves that do not really preach the kernel of the message. Frequently, preachers who write or preach without first outlining spend too much time getting to the heart of the matter.

J. Write a Full Homily Text

If an outline is the skeleton of a homily, the full text is the flesh and bones. Outlines tend to be a series of ideas and themes, indicating what preachers will talk about. Written texts help preachers plan not only what they will say, but how they will say it. Some preachers feel that a full text inhibits them. This method suggests that preachers at least experiment with writing full texts to determine whether they find themselves more fully prepared than when they preach only from an outline. If preachers honestly determine they are better prepared without a written text, they should not write one. The real issue is that preachers prepare themselves as well as they possibly can to proclaim the word of God.

K. Tape the Homily

The written word communicates to the eye, the spoken word speaks to the ear. A homily that will be heard, rather than read, by the congregation is most effective when it is written in a style that communicates orally. When preachers finish writing the text, it is a good idea to read the text aloud using a tape recorder. Listening to the tape helps determine how the message communicates to the ear.

L. Internalize the Message

If the previous step shows that the homily is effective oral communication, preachers now allow the message to preach to them. Since preachers are also listeners to God's word, this final step is an opportunity to allow the word to sink in, to become good news for those who will proclaim it to others.

4. Using Notes in the Pulpit

Once a homily text is complete, preachers have one more decision to make. Some will choose to read the full homily manuscript at the pulpit. Some will glance at the manuscript occasionally while trying to keep eye contact with the congregation. Others may preach from an outline or list of key words or phrases. Each of these strategies has advantages, especially in terms of content recall and exact phrasing of well-crafted sentences.

If the homily is the word of a believer witnessing to other believers, homily manuscripts and even brief notes can become a barrier between preachers and the congregation. An elderly parishioner once asked her pastor, "Father, if you need notes to remember what you have to say, how do you expect an old lady like me to remember the message?" Her question goes beyond simply recalling the homily. A more important issue is, What does heavy reliance on notes or a full homily text communicate to the congregation? Preachers are witnesses of the God whom they have met in the scriptures. Preachers proclaim their belief to other believers. This special nature and purpose of the liturgical homily suggests that once preachers have listened and believed the message, they might risk leaving the text or notes in the sacristy as they proclaim this good news to other believers.

Further Reading

Brusatti, Louis T. "The Primordial Word: Preaching, Poetry, and Pastoral Presence." In *In the Company of Preachers*. Aquinas Institute of Theology. Collegeville, Minn.: Liturgical Press, 1993, pp. 210-26.

Burghardt, Walter J. *Preaching: The Art and the Craft*. New York: Paulist Press, 1987 (especially pages 1-42 dealing with imagination in preaching).

Notes

1. This poem was written around 1980 by a student at Kenrick Seminary, St. Louis. It is reproduced with permission of the author.

2. Don M. Wardlaw, ed., *Learning Preaching: Understanding & Participating in the Process* (Lincoln, Ill.: Lincoln Christian, 1989), p. 75.

3. Clarence Thomson, "The Right Brain Language of Power," in *Preaching Better*, ed. Frank J. McNulty (Mahwah, N.J.: Paulist Press, 1985), pp. 87-88.

4. Thomas Kane, ed., *Teaching Advanced Homiletics: Proceedings of*

the Weston Summer Institute, vol. 3 (Newton, Mass.: Sophia Press, 1994), p. 75.

5. Walter J. Burghardt, Address. Aquinas Great Preacher of the Year Award. St. Louis, 28 April 1995.

6. Paul Scott Wilson, "Imagination," in *Concise Encyclopedia of Preaching*, ed. William H. Willimon and Richard Lischer (Louisville: Westminster/Knox, 1995), pp. 266-69.

7. Wilson, p. 267.

8. Walter Brueggemann, *The Prophetic Imagination* (Philadelphia: Fortress Press, 1989), p. 13.

9. Wilson, p. 267.

10. Wilson, p. 267.

11. Karl Rahner, "Priest and Poet," in *Theological Investigations* III, trans. Karl H. and Boniface Kruger (Baltimore: Helicon Press, 1967), p. 317.

12. Brewster Ghiselin, ed., *The Creative Process* (New York: New American Library, 1952), pp. 11-32.

13. Ghiselin, p. 14.

14. Ghiselin, p. 14.

15. Ghiselin, p. 21.

16. Ghiselin, p. 26.

17. Walter J. Burghardt, "From Study to Proclamation," in *A New Look at Preaching*, ed. John Burke (Wilmington, Del.: Michael Glazier, 1983), p. 27.

18. Anne Lamott, *Bird by Bird: Some Instructions on Writing and Life* (New York: Pantheon, 1994), pp. 97-102.

19. Lamott, pp. 133-44.

20. Wardlaw, p. 81.

21. Douglas E. Oakman, "Was Jesus a Peasant?: Implications for Reading the Samaritan Story (Luke 10:30-35),"*Biblical Theology Bulletin* 22 (1992): 117-25.

22. Paul VI, Address to the Members of the *Consilium de Laicis* (October 2, 1974) *Acta Apostolicae Sedis* 66 (1974): 568.

23. Lamott, p. 19.

Chapter Four

Preaching the Scriptures

Do We Preach *on* God's Word or *from* God's Word?

1. Information or Transformation?

Scripture scholars and preachers need each other in the ministry of the word. Scholars enlighten those who seek understanding, but they do not necessarily help the word enliven and feed the faith of believers. On the other hand, preachers who do not seriously study the word may be able to present interesting talks, but their eloquent words lack the power of God's living word. Preaching that goes beyond explaining the readings breaks open the word and "invites the assembly to consider that word in light of communal and personal worldviews."[1] Preachers exercise a genuine ministry of study when they delve into the depths of the word in order to allow the word to speak to the faithful. Their ultimate goal is not information, but transformation.

Augustine wrote one of the earliest works on the preacher's responsibility to study the scriptures. Although he did not have the advantage of contemporary biblical interpretation methods, he was passionate about the importance of careful study. For Augustine, the goal of scholarship was to increase not one's store of knowledge, but one's faith. He shows his appreciation for the way that studying the scriptures leads to holiness: "Whoever, therefore, thinks that he understands the divine Scriptures or any part of them so that it does not build the double love of God and of our neighbor does not understand it at all."[2]

This chapter deals with the *interpretation of scripture*. Readers will not be full-fledged scripture scholars after reading this brief treatment. This chapter is intended to reaffirm the importance of rooting homilies in God's word. It begins by describing the preacher's role as proclaiming, rather than explaining, the scriptures. Second, it describes historical criticism and social science criticism. The chapter concludes with several practical guidelines for preachers as they move from the scriptures to the homily.

2. The Scriptures As the Source of Preaching

Explanation versus Proclamation
An earlier discussion of worship as first-order language pointed out that homilies are *from* the scriptures, not *on* the scriptures. This is one of the major ways that a homily as proclamation differs from an explanation. Exegesis is essential for preaching, but exegesis is not preaching itself. The following examples illustrate the difference between explaining and proclaiming. Ezekiel describes the Lord leading the prophet out into a vast field of dried bones that evoke a sense of Israel's spiritual despair.

> Thus says the Lord God: O my people, I will open your graves and have you rise from them and bring you back to the land of Israel. Then you shall know that I am the Lord, when I open your graves and have you rise from them, O my people! I will put my spirit in you that you may live, and I will settle you upon your land; thus you shall know that I am the Lord. I have promised, and I will do it, says the Lord.
>
> Ezekiel 37:12-14

Example: Explanation
> This passage is sometimes misunderstood as a description of the resurrection from the dead. It is especially tempting to draw an eschatological theme from verse 12 in which God says through the prophet, "I will open your graves and have you rise from them...." This book, which describes incidents in the sixth century B.C.E., predates any notion of bodily resurrection and eternal life. This pericope speaks of new life for the living, not for the dead.
>
> The prophet Ezekiel is aware of the utter discouragement of the Israelites during the Babylonian exile. He

stands in a vast field strewn with bones. It was likely the site of a great battle. The image of dry, lifeless bones is an apt description of the hopelessness the Israelites feel in their separation from their native land. Bones suggest the image of stamina. We are familiar with the expression, "Show some backbone." The people certainly lacked backbone at the moment. They no doubt wondered whether their God was even aware of their plight. The prophet offers new hope.

Example: Proclamation

Do you enjoy ghost stories? In the movie *Poltergeist*, an expert in paranormal research offered a fascinating description of ghosts. According to her, ghosts are persons who lived dull, boring existences all their lives. They mindlessly followed the same routines over and over. When they died they did not even realize they should have moved on to the next life. They just continue to follow their old routines, oblivious of their death.

I have never seen a ghost, but I have seen some people who would make excellent ghosts someday. It is sad to see a hopeless, lifeless person. The Israelites in exile were just such a people. They had been forced from their beloved homeland and brought to a strange place of slavery. I imagine they did not stand very straight when they walked. I see them as ambling along very slowly, perhaps stooped over, lacking backbone.

Onto this scene steps God's prophet, Ezekiel. He stands on a battlefield strewn with dry, lifeless bones and sees the plight of his own people. The prophet will not allow the people to be living ghosts. Through his mouth the Lord proclaims new life, new spirit for this people. The dry bones will grow flesh and dance around. The people will once again live. God's breath is life!

The Bible: Not a Handbook

The scriptures tell the story of God choosing to be immersed in the world of men and women. The Hebrew scriptures recount how

God formed a chosen people from a group of nomads. The Christian scriptures present Jesus of Nazareth, the Son of God, the savior. The Bible is about God's world and the human world becoming one world. To faithfully proclaim the scriptures, preachers preach the person of God, not only teachings *about* God. Above all, the Bible must not be reduced to a moral or catechetical handbook. To reduce the scriptures to a mere set of prescripts is to squeeze the rich life out of God's word.

Chapter One has already dealt with the unfortunate practice of preaching directly from the catechism rather than from the scriptures. Some preachers too quickly latch on to a theme from one or more of the Sunday readings, then set God's word aside as they construct a teaching from the catechism. The *Catechism of the Catholic Church* can be an excellent resource for informing a homily, but it is not the source of the liturgical homily. The catechism that explains God is not the Bible, which is the word of God.

Preaching on Morality

The same caution holds true when preaching about morality. Although the scriptures contain clear and specific exhortations for moral living, the scriptures are not a moral handbook. Charles Bouchard, the Dominican moral theologian, makes an important distinction between preaching moral laws and preaching Jesus who calls men and women to be moral persons. The scriptures, even when dealing with morality, do not simply tell me what rules I must follow, but challenge me to ask, "What kind of person should I be?"[3]

In Matthew 5:20-26, for example, Jesus teaches his disciples that holiness goes beyond minimal observance of the law. Everyone knows murder is a violation of God's law. Jesus goes further in teaching that believers must not even grow angry with a brother or sister. A preacher who uses this passage as a moral handbook might be tempted to launch into a list of sins against charity. Jesus is not supplying a new list of behaviors, but calling disciples to become new persons. Some may see the distinction as unimportant. After all, if people end up following the law, what difference does it make whether homilies tell them which laws to follow or help them to be renewed persons called to follow the law of Christ? The issue becomes pivotal when we consider grace. If merely telling people what they should believe and do will make them better persons, then people do not need Jesus, since they can save themselves. If we become new persons when we allow Jesus to be the power in our lives, then the rules alone are not enough. A later chapter dealing with the preacher as prophet explores this question in greater detail.

Focusing on God in the Scriptures

Authentic preaching focuses on God's activity in the scriptures. Homilies that attend only to the words and deeds of the various human characters end up being mere thematic lectures. As Bouchard notes, "Every scriptural passage, because it is the word of God, has within it the potential to illumine any topic."[4] Because the scriptures bring God and believers into contact with one another, individual passages transcend mere themes. Luke describes how a father forgives his wayward prodigal son who has squandered the inheritance and now returns home. This story is more than a lesson about parents forgiving children. The word presents a forgiving God. A homily on this gospel need not be limited to forgiveness. Preachers first focus on how God is present in the scripture passage. Only after getting in touch with the Lord do preachers move to the next step of linking the particular reading to some aspect of the congregation's lives.

The Context of a Passage

Public persons often complain that they are quoted out of context. A congressperson, for example, might say at a press conference, "We must get the poor off the streets and out of the alleys of our cities!" As an isolated statement, this might sound like a heartless comment. If the original context was an impassioned plea for creating more jobs and decent housing for the homeless so that they are not forced to live on the streets, the quotation takes on an entirely different tone. Every Lectionary reading is taken out of a larger context. Each selection is the result of an editor's decision that a reading can stand on its own. Most readings suffer when they are preached out of context.

Sheep-Gate or Shepherd?

The gospel for the Fourth Sunday of Easter (Year A) is John 10:1-

10. Jesus calls himself the gate through which the sheep—the people—may enter to find safety. If preachers consider this reading on its own, and not in its original context, they might preach Jesus as a good shepherd who knows his sheep and cares for each of them. The homily may be a consoling message of how special we are in God's eyes. The consoling message of the Good Shepherd belongs to the later verses in this chapter. This first section is not about Jesus as a shepherd, but as a sheep-gate who stands in contrast to a group of self-important religious leaders who claimed to be able to lead others in God's ways.

If the passage is seen in its larger context, the reader will note that in John 9, Jesus cures a man born blind. The miracle concerns more than physical healing. The cure drew the attention of some religious leaders who questioned the man in a dramatic trial scene. The formerly blind man begins to see the true nature of Jesus. The more his eyes are opened, the more the eyes of the religious leaders are closed. In their stubbornness they refuse to believe. At the conclusion of the chapter the man meets Jesus and bows in worship as a profession of faith. The one who was blind now sees in a new way. The ones who had once been able to see now have become blind.

The beginning of John 10 shows Jesus to be the true sheep-gate, unlike those blind guides who were supposed to lead people to God. They themselves had refused to see. How could they guide anyone else? There is only one person who can lead others to the kingdom of God; only in Jesus will people find salvation. The homily will be richer when the reading is examined in its fuller context.

3. Historical Criticism

As previously noted, *Fulfilled in Your Hearing* (n. 20) calls preachers to "interpret the human situation through the Scriptures." Before preachers can interpret the contemporary human situation, they must be able to interpret scriptures that were written within a cultural situation very different from our own. Complicating the process is the fact that the scriptures were written by "inconsiderate" human authors. The authors of the scriptures knew nothing of our present world, nor did they have any need to explain their own world to us. Because their first readers shared the same culture, biblical authors did not need to explain details that modern scholars must discover. All authors, ancient and modern, are inconsiderate in this sense.[5]

Computer manuals offer an illustration of inconsiderate writing. If a computer programmer writes a technical manual to be used by other programmers, he or she would not hesitate to write, "After REMing out the cache statement in the autoexec.bat file, remember to reboot before proceeding." Inexperienced computer users would find that statement thoroughly baffling. The author is inconsiderate of the average reader, but is considerate of readers versed in technology. If the programmer explained every detail of the instruction so that a novice could understand, the text would actually be inconsiderate of the intended audience. Modern readers must not expect ancient scriptures to speak clearly to our world. *We must enter the ancient world.* This is the first task of scripture study.

The World behind the Text

In 1994 the Pontifical Biblical Commission published "The Interpretation of the Bible in the Church."[6] The commission reasserted the importance of historical criticism (which it calls the historical-critical method) as indispensable for interpreting the scriptures. The document also describes a rich variety of approaches that ask of the text questions not posed by historical criticism.

This chapter does not attempt to describe all of the many types of biblical interpretation. We will briefly examine historical criticism, since it is an essential tool for interpreting the scriptures. A large part of the chapter discusses social science criticism, which offers fresh insights for interpretation. It is hoped that these brief observations will encourage preachers to explore the topic through further reading. Biblical interpretation, like preaching itself, demands lifelong learning.

> Historical criticism looks to the world behind the text. Scriptural texts and traditions developed in stages throughout their history. The human authors entrusted with communicating God's word depended upon many ancient sources and traditions. Historical criticism is therefore a diachronic process. It studies the way scriptures have developed across time ("The Interpretation of the Bible in the Church," p. 500).

Joseph Fitzmyer has written an extensive commentary on the Pontifical Biblical Commission's document. He traces the roots of historical criticism back to the ancient Greeks who used some elements of the method to reconstruct the best texts of Homer's *Iliad* and *Odyssey*. Later, Jerome and Augustine used early forms of this criticism to study the scriptures. The approach became more sophisticated by the time of the Renaissance, when scholars in many disciplines were concerned about returning to original sources. During the sixteenth-century Reformation both Luther and Calvin employed elements of the method as a reaction to the medieval allegorical interpretation of the scriptures. The concern for developing a scientific method of examining the world behind the text continued to develop. It took a dramatic turn in the nineteenth century when the hieroglyphics on the Rosetta stone were at last deciphered. This discovery allowed scholars entry to ancient Assyrian, Babylonian and Sumerian literature. Biblical interpretation could show more clearly than ever how the scriptures made use of literature from the ancient world.[7]

Fitzmyer notes that the historical-critical method came under suspicion at a certain point in the history of the Catholic Church. Pope Leo XIII established the Pontifical Biblical Commission in 1902 with the stated purpose of promoting biblical scholarship. The commission, while not actually condemning historical criticism, was influential in discouraging a too critical study of the Bible.[8] The 1994 statement from the Pontifical Biblical Commission in effect exonerated the historical-critical method, calling it "the indispensable method for the scientific study of the meaning of ancient texts" ("The Interpretation of the Bible in the Church," p. 500).

The "Problem" of the Man without the Wedding Garment

The historical-critical method is considered indispensable because it begins in the world that first produced the text. When dealing with ancient biblical texts there is always a danger that one's own world will cloud understanding. Matthew 22:1-14 tells the story of a king who gave a wedding banquet for his son. When the invited refused to attend, the king sent his servants out to invite all they met, the bad as well as the good. When the king entered the banquet hall, he saw that one of the guests was not wearing a wedding garment. The king had the man bound and thrown out into the night. Modern readers are often perplexed by this story. Who goes around in the streets dressed for a wedding? If the servants were snatching potential guests from the streets, of course they would not be dressed up. Contemporary readers also wonder why the king showed so little compassion for a poor person who could not afford a wedding garment. These and other questions arise when one approaches the text with the values of one's own world. Historical criticism requires readers to set aside their own world of experience and ask how the text came to be and what the text meant to its first audience.

When readers enter the world of the text, they discover that this story is a parable. Parables are intended to turn the reader's world upside down. They cause the reader to set aside misconceptions about God; they also challenge the reader to accept God on God's own terms. Characters in parables are not meant to be models for contemporary behavior. This section of Matthew is a parable that describes the kingdom. Not all who are invited choose to come. Those who do decide to walk in the ways of the Lord are expected to undergo personal conversion. The wedding garment in this passage is a sign of that interior conversion. In the earliest accounts of Christian baptism, the newly baptized adult came out of the waters and was clothed in a white tunic. This garment was a symbol that the newly baptized person was ready to put on Christ. The man in this story who would not wear a wedding garment showed his obstinacy. He was not willing to put on Christ.

Historical criticism also asks about the context of the passage. What has preceded the passage? What follows it? Does the book of the Bible from which the selection comes have a specific purpose? These and other questions about the original form and purpose of the passage allow the reader to discover the world behind the text.

Historicity of the Bible

Historical criticism is indispensable because it deals with the historicity of the text. Biblical faith is a faith that rests on events, not on abstract ideas. This does not mean that the Bible is a history book in the contemporary sense of that term. The human authors of the Bible were not historians in the way we think about historians, but they did write about historical events. Scripture records the history of God at work in people and events from creation to the final days. To strip this history from the scriptures is to remove the faith value of the word. Readers using historical criticism seek to understand the text in terms of "its own time, place, and culture. In historical interpretation one tries to answer the questions: Who wrote this text? to whom? when? where? and why?"[9]

Applying the Method

Using historical criticism, preachers begin studying the readings for the Sunday liturgy by first setting aside their own worldview and preconceptions as much as possible. They read each reading with fresh ears, as if this were the first time they ever saw this particular passage. After listening carefully to the text, they answer the following questions:

- What is the origin of the text? Who wrote it, to whom, and why?
- What is the context of the passage? What has occurred before and after the Lectionary section? How might this context shed light on the meaning of the passage?
- What is the form of the text? Is it historical narrative? A parable? Prophecy? Epistle? Apocalyptic? Does the form itself suggest anything about the meaning of the text?
- What did the first audience probably think or do when they first heard the text?

Having posed these and other questions from the world behind the text, preachers can begin formulating some answers by making use of scholarly resources that employ historical criticism. Among the best known are *The New Jerome Biblical Commentary* and *The Anchor Bible Dictionary*.

The questions a preacher asks of the text in historical criticism are foundational, but not exhaustive. Preachers may examine the scriptures through many lenses. As already mentioned, it is not the intention of this chapter to present the entire field of biblical interpretation. Readers who would like an introduction to the wide variety of interpretive methods can consult the Pontifical Biblical

Commission's article, "The Interpretation of the Bible in the Church."

4. Social Science Criticism

Like historical criticism, social science criticism looks to the world behind the text. This approach involves further questions of the text in light of the sociological and cultural systems that existed when the authors wrote the text. Social science criticism deals with issues that help modern readers appreciate how biblical authors as well as the first readers and hearers looked at themselves as members of the community.

Gaps in the Scripture Text

The Christian scriptures were produced within a "high-context" society. The people living in first-century eastern Mediterranean society shared so much of their lives in common that they immediately understood what another intended in oral and written communication.[10] The authors felt no need to explain the commonly held beliefs, attitudes and social conventions that seem very foreign to contemporary readers. As a result, the scriptures are filled with large gaps in the text. This is another symptom of the "inconsiderate" authors mentioned earlier. Biblical authors could not be expected to write for modern readers who know a radically different social experience.

How the Scriptures Look at Healing

The way gospel society looked at disease and illness, for example, provides a good argument for the value of social science criticism. Bruce Malina and other advocates of this method argue that healing is a culturally biased concept. Modern Western medicine places high value on curing specific diseases. The people in the gospel world would find this notion baffling. For them, the issue was not disease, but illness. "Illness is not so much a biomedical matter as it is a social one...a matter of deviance from cultural norms and values."[11] When people came to Jesus for healing, the issue was not diseased organs as much as illness that made the person a social and religious outcast. To be healed went beyond restoring body functions; it meant being restored to full membership in the community. When Jesus healed lepers he gave them healthy skin, but more importantly he restored them to full membership in the community.

Biblical authors did not explain the difference between disease and illness, nor did they explain the ramifications of healing that restored one's place in society. Their contemporaries understood what was involved when Jesus healed someone. Modern readers will likely miss the underlying message of the healing stories due to gaps in the text. Preachers who appreciate the first-century eastern Mediterranean notion of illness have a richer understanding of what Jesus did in the lives of those he healed. These preachers also have an advantage of proclaiming what Jesus does in healing people who today are separated from the community through sin.

Social Science Criticism and the Samaritan Story

Social science criticism offers a fresh perspective on a very old story, the Samaritan in the gospel of Luke. Chapter Three of this book introduced a social science interpretation of this story, in the discussion of the Five Fundamental Questions. This section delves deeper into that interpretation and presents a sample homily. Most preachers treat this section of the gospel as an example story, illustrating how we ought to treat our neighbors. Douglas Oakman argues that once the reader enters the social world that Luke knew, the story is not so much about how we ought to act, but about how God acts toward us. Oakman's unique perspective on this story is described in an article provocatively titled, "Was Jesus a Peasant?: Implications for Reading the Samaritan Story (Luke 10:30-35)."[12] Read the gospel story once again with fresh ears:

There was a scholar of the law who stood up to test Jesus and said, "Teacher, what must I do to inherit eternal life?" Jesus said to him, "What is written in the law? How do you read it?" He said in reply, "You shall love the Lord, your God, with all your heart, with all your being, with all your strength, and with all your mind, and your neighbor as yourself." He replied to him, "You have answered correctly; do this and you will live."

But because he wished to justify himself, he said to Jesus, "And who is my neighbor?" Jesus replied, "A man fell victim to robbers as he went down from Jerusalem to Jericho. They stripped and beat him and went off leaving him half-dead. A priest happened to be going down that road, but when he saw him, he passed by on the opposite side. Likewise a Levite came to the place, and when he saw him, he passed by on the opposite side. But a Samaritan traveler who came upon him was moved with compassion at the sight. He approached the victim, poured oil and wine over his wounds and bandaged them. Then he lifted him up on his own animal, took him to an inn, and cared for him. The next day he took out two silver coins and gave them to the innkeeper with the instruction, 'Take care of him. If you spend more than what I have given you, I shall repay you on my way back.' Which of these three, in your opinion, was neighbor to the robbers' victim?" He answered, "The one who treated him with mercy." Jesus said to him, "Go and do likewise."

The Social World of the Samaritan

The final verse of the gospel might lead the reader to conclude that it is a mere example story: The listener should go and do as the Samaritan did. Oakman argues that this final verse was not part of the original material. The story in its purest form (without this verse) is a parable that turns the status quo on its head. The story is really about a "foolish Samaritan"; it challenges the listener to reevaluate narrow presuppositions about what the kingdom of God is like.[13] Essential to Oakman's interpretation of this story is his conviction that Jesus was a peasant artisan telling the story to other peasants.

Peasants in the Time of Jesus

The peasants living at the time of Jesus had much in common with the poor and the homeless that we are familiar with in our own society. They lacked full control over their lives. They were rural people, not necessarily farmers, who produced what they needed for self-sufficiency. They were forced to give their surplus to overlords. The overlords kept the peasants indebted to them through heavy borrowing. In the Judea and Galilee of the gospels, the Romans exploited these peasants. Peasants had little love for the rich merchants who, they believed, grew rich at the expense of the poor.[14]

Jesus, then, may be considered a peasant artisan, according to Oakman's description of peasantry. Jesus' many references to plants and farming show that he knew agrarian life well. Like most in his world, Jesus was also subject to overlords. His ministry was exercised in the cause of peasants.[15] It is obvious from the gospels that Jesus identified with the poor, although he also had access to the homes of the influential.

The Samaritan

In the eyes of the peasants who heard Jesus tell the story, the Samaritan was far from being a *good* Samaritan. He was a merchant rich enough to travel, trading in oil and wine carried by a pack animal. He brought the injured man to an inn, the usual haven for traders. In short, he represented all that was oppressive to the peasants. If that were not enough, he did not have the good sense to stay among his own people. To care for one's own was acceptable social behavior. To care for one's enemies was pure foolishness.[16] There are other details in this story that give the gospel new meaning when read through the lens of social science criticism.

In this sample homily, the phrases in brackets at the start of each section provide indications to the development of the homily.

5. Sample Homily: The Foolish Samaritan

[Being Good to God] A friend recently returned from a trip to Mexico with a delightful story to tell me. He had wandered into a little village church where he was immediately drawn to a lavish, gold-covered side altar. He noticed a small dedication plate at the base of the altar. He slowly read aloud the old Spanish inscription: "This altar was built because God has been very, very good to Señor Vargas. And Señor Vargas has been very, very good to God."

[Do We Try to Appease God?] I had a very hearty laugh when I heard this story. It is charming to realize that years ago some wealthy Mexican patron needed to remind God that he, Señor Vargas, was good enough to donate this expensive altar. I laughed until I remembered several embarrassing incidents in my own spiritual journey when I have tried to appease God. At times I have promised God that if things went the way I was praying they would, I would in turn be more dedicated to prayer or be more charitable or generous to others. There where also times when I was especially generous—times when no bargaining was involved. I was asking nothing of God. I was simply trying to be more prayerful or charitable in the hope that God would be pleased with my efforts. Have any of you ever bargained with God? Or have you tried to be a better person to please God in order to win a special favor? I have never met an honest person who has denied that he or she has tried to please God and win God's favor. And yet God's word today tells us we do not earn God's love—it is pure gift.

[Beyond an Example Story] The gospel we have just heard is usually titled the Story of the Good Samaritan. The priest and Levite who were concerned with their own external observance of the law passed by the beaten traveler. But the Samaritan alone was good enough, generous enough to help the poor unfortunate. We should be like the Samaritan. And that, of course, is true enough. We should love others, especially when it demands a great deal of effort from us. Is that all this gospel is saying? Or is there a meaning beyond the obvious lesson about charity? Let us take a closer look at the characters in the story. Perhaps in our imaginations we could stand in the crowd and observe how others are listening to Jesus.

[Responses from Jesus' Audience] Who were the people listening with rapt attention as Jesus wove the story of robbers, villains and heroes? There must have been priests and Levites in the audience. In fact, the one who prompts the story is a lawyer. As these professional holy men listened to Jesus, we can almost see them nodding in agreement as the priest and the Levite walk past the beaten man. And why do the holy men agree that they should not stop? Suppose the beaten man turned out to be dead? If so, the priest and Levite would have incurred ritual impurity by touching a corpse. That meant they would not be able to participate in Temple services. And furthermore, what if the robbers who beat this man were waiting in the bushes to pounce on do-gooders who might stop to help? Yes, the sensible thing was to keep moving.

[The Foolish Samaritan] Along comes the Samaritan. I don't know if you realized something as you are standing in this crowd listening to Jesus today. Have you noticed the way many in the crowd are dressed? Most of the people listening with us are poor. They are dressed in old, tattered clothes. And, frankly, they smell a bit. Have you noticed? These poor are there because Jesus is one of them. He lives among them, and works hard with his hands as they do. These poor know that the Samaritan Jesus speaks about is not one of them. He is one of the rich and famous. He has a pack animal to carry the oil and wine that he is going to sell at market. He can afford the luxurious gesture of pouring oil and wine into the wounds of the beaten man. Already the simple folks are uneasy that the Samaritan is getting involved. It is OK to take care of one's own. Jews should take care of Jews, just as Samaritans should take care of Samaritans. Let the Samaritan stay with his own kind.

And then this foolish Samaritan does something truly outrageous. After dressing the man's wounds, he puts him on the pack animal and brings him to an inn. This is not a Holiday Inn. This is a place for traveling salesmen. Innkeepers are not model citizens. No, they are a rough bunch. What does this Samaritan do now? He leaves the man at the inn, gives money to the innkeeper and says, "Take care of him and I will pay whatever it has cost you when I come back this way." The innkeeper, if he is true to his nature, will keep the sick man hostage and run up a big bill. He is no fool. The Samaritan is the fool. Most of the people standing next to us in the crowd are laughing out of control at this final, foolish act of the stupid Samaritan.

[God Loves Generously, Perhaps Foolishly] So how do you and I react as we hear this story? Can we see that the Samaritan actually shows us the face of God? Jesus is telling us about the kingdom and what kind of God we have who invites us into the kingdom. God turns things upside down and does not give people what they deserve. God gives people more than they deserve. God hands us a blank check, doing whatever is necessary to draw us into the kingdom, even to the point of asking an only son to die on a cross.

[Are We Bystanders in the Kingdom?] Does all this mean that we stand back with folded arms and wait for God to do all the work? If God is foolish enough to hand us a blank check, why should we be out trying to do anything? That, of course, is not the point of this gospel story. Clearly Jesus was not praising the priest and Levite who walked on when they saw a brother in need. They were not acting the way God acts. Although the kingdom is God's gift, and although we can never earn God's love, we are called to jump into the life of the kingdom with full energy.

[We Live in a Broken World] You and I may not have the opportunity to rescue people beaten by robbers, although that is certainly not out of the question in today's broken world. This story is not only about victims of assault. If you have not read the Sunday paper yet, try this test. See how quickly you can find a news story about someone who was murdered yesterday. How many stories deal with war or terrorism? Are there any stories describing the poor? We don't really have to take the test. We already know we live in a very broken world. Jesus asks that we care for the least of our brothers and sisters. It can be frustrating, can't it? Do you sometimes throw your hands in the air and ask, "What can I possibly do about all this?"

[Relying on God's Strength] This is the good news from today's gospel. We don't have to do it all ourselves. In fact, if we try to pull ourselves up by our spiritual boot-

straps, we are bound to fail. The kingdom of God is ultimately God's work. We don't have to run around doing
good little deeds so the Lord will think more highly of us.
The Lord who loves us enough to write blank checks, if
that's what it takes, will work in us so that God's love
spreads among those called to the kingdom.

[The Eucharist] The Eucharist we now share is one of
the best ways for us to live in God's kingdom of justice
here and now. We have been called to enjoy the fullness
of that kingdom some day, but not today. Today we are
still on the road toward the kingdom. Our lives are about
showing God's generous gift of the kingdom to others.
We do this by the way we treat others, even if we have
never met them. Perhaps in this sometimes cynical
world, people might consider us foolish for having such
deep concern for others. If so, today's gospel tells us that
we are in good company. Let this Eucharist be the food
that sustains us to show the face of God to all in need.

The homily about the "foolish" Samaritan would have been very
different if the preacher had not entered the social and cultural
world of the author and audience. Our own world admires, if not
always emulates, the Samaritan as an example of charity. The term
"good Samaritan" is part of the English language. An organization
of recreational vehicle owners calls itself the Good Sam Club. Members pledge to help travelers in difficulty. Many of the peasants listening to Jesus considered the Samaritan to be a fool. Is the gospel
primarily about being a do-gooder, or about a generous, foolish
God? Preachers who allow themselves to enter the first-century
eastern Mediterranean world are in for many fresh insights.

6. The Biblical World Speaks to Our World

Dyadic Personality

One of the major differences between the world of the gospels
and our world is the sense of self. Modern Western people place a
high value on self-esteem. Our afternoon television programs are
filled with people eager to talk about their deepest feelings and concerns. Biblical characters show very little sense of the inner self.

Notice how rarely there is only one character "on stage" in biblical narratives. People in the world of the gospels received their sense of self from being immersed in the group. Social-science critics refer to this characteristic as *dyadic personality*.[17]

Consequences for Preaching

Preachers who are aware of how the group gives a sense of identity and self-esteem to gospel characters will begin to notice another level to many gospel stories. Jesus readily dined with persons considered to be sinners. In our culture most people are reluctant to be seen in the company of "the wrong people." People in the gospels associated with their own kind, especially at mealtime. Their peer group helped them to know who they were. But Jesus went well beyond that. If he dines with sinners, what is he saying about the extraordinary steps he will take to reach out to others?

In a world of dyadic personalities, people were expected to behave according to the norms of their trade. Farmers acted like farmers, carpenters acted like carpenters. What did it mean for Jesus the artisan to start behaving like a teacher? Where did he get such wisdom? Where did Jesus get the authority to tell the Samaritan story that criticizes the sensible actions of the priest and Levite? Why did the Samaritan not stay with his own people instead of meddling in the affairs of others?

Zones of Activity

Characters in the gospels did not talk about inner feelings, attitudes or emotions. They would have no idea what to do in a therapist's office. When first-century biblical people needed to express their inner selves they referred to one of three zones of the body. Chapter One already discussed these three zones of activity concerning the cure of the blind beggar, Bartimaeus. The reader may wish to review the section that describes the zones of the mouth-ears, the eyes-heart, and the hands-feet. Activities that involve these zones are outward expressions of one's inner soul. They serve as metaphors for what the people could express in no other way. The eyes-heart zone expresses the character's inner thoughts and emotions, the mouth-ears zone expresses the communication that enters and leaves the body, and the hands-feet zone expresses purposeful activity.[18]

Consequences for Preaching

The gospels are filled with references to these three zones of the body. Since the world of the scriptures lacks the vocabulary to discuss complex inner thoughts, emotions and feelings, the three zones tell the reader what is happening within persons. Consider the healing stories, for example. As wonderful as it is that someone once physically blind can now see, the gospel is saying much more. Jesus has opened the mind to know him and the heart to accept him as Lord.

When the Pharisees criticize Jesus' disciples for eating with unwashed hands, they were concerned about what the disciples were allowing to enter their mouths. Will their neglect of the custom make them impure? Jesus responded, "Nothing that enters one from outside can defile that person; but the things that come out from within are what defile" (Mark 7:15). Persons in this culture were very concerned about what entered the body through the mouth and ears. These orifices were boundaries against impurity. Impure food and speech could render the person impure. Jesus challenges his hearers to think anew about what constitutes impurity by calling them to look less to the external and more to what is inside a person: "All these evils come from within and they defile" (Mark 7:23).

Preachers who appreciate these zones of activity will also notice how often the hands and feet are used to express purposeful activity. Throughout the Bible, religious leaders lay hands on others as an expression of passing special power and authority to them. The healing of Bartimaeus (Mark 10:46-52) involves more than the zone of the eyes-heart. At the same moment Jesus cures Bartimaeus he tells him, "Go your way; your faith has saved you." Was Jesus telling him to get out of his presence? A social science critic would see this as a call for Bartimaeus to set out and do something with his new sight, his new faith. There is no time to stand around. It is also significant that Bartimaeus sets his feet to follow Jesus. He now sees where to go with his life.

The story of the Samaritan refers to these zones that describe interior attitudes and emotions. The gospel says that the priest and Levite "saw" the man who was beaten by robbers. A person who sees with the eyes has also seen with the mind and heart. Their eyes—that is, their minds and hearts—were closed. Both the priest and Levite then "went on." Clearly their "purposeful activity" did not include the needs of someone who was ritually unclean.

Honor/Shame

Honor and shame are core values for the people of Jesus' world. It may seem strange to hear that shame is a value, but certain types of shame were considered desirable. Honor and shame were expressed differently by men and women. For males, honor associated with strength, power and virtue was everything. A male was publicly shamed if he was seen as weak or vulnerable. On the other hand, it was positive for a man to "have shame," since it meant he was concerned about his honor. Our culture is familiar with the expression, "Have you no shame?" Females in biblical times had honor if they were the guardians of shame, that is, if they took care to preserve privacy and purity.[19]

To challenge someone's honor in public was very serious; it was an attack on what people valued most highly. Further, people in this culture believed honor to exist in limited quantities. There was only so much honor to go around. If one person had a certain amount of honor, it meant another person had that much less honor.[20] The notion that there is a finite supply of honor is foreign to modern readers. In our world many people can simultaneously possess great honor. Readers must take care not to impose our notion of honor on the scriptures.

Since honor and shame (in its positive sense) are such core values, readers can expect to see these concerns permeate the gospels. Jesus often faced public challenges to his honor from enemies attempting to trap him in his speech. This introduces another insight from social science criticism. By engaging in challenge and riposte, one party seeks to acquire the honor of another. The exchange involves four stages: 1) someone makes a public statement of honor by word or gesture; 2) another party publicly challenges this honor; 3) the first party reacts to this challenge with a riposte that affirms one's own honor and challenges the honor of the second party; 4) the people witnessing the public challenge-riposte pronounce their verdict of who won the challenge.[21]

John 8:12-59 offers a clear example of challenge-riposte between Jesus and the Pharisees. Jesus calls himself the light of the world. This is his public statement of honor. The Pharisees challenge his honor by saying that nobody can be his own witness. Jesus returns with the riposte that his witness is valid since he knows where he came from and where he is going. Furthermore, Jesus says that the Pharisees do not know his origins or final goal. The chapter continues with a heated exchange between Jesus and the Pharisees. They are not arguing Christology, but discussing honor. Jesus calls his disciples to see him as the one sent from God. To recognize this honor is to believe.

Consequences for Preaching

Jesus stood on a mountainside and proclaimed something rather extraordinary to a people who considered honor to be the most precious thing they could possess. So important was honor that these people fought in public gatherings to possess honor that was in limited supply. To this people Jesus proclaimed that those are blessed who are poor in spirit, insulted, persecuted and slandered (Matthew 5:1-12). This is the same Jesus who washed the feet of his followers as he knelt before them at the Last Supper. After washing their feet Jesus asked, "Do you realize what I have done for you?" (John 13:12) Jesus has turned the notion of honor upside down. Honor is no longer a matter of lording over others. Instead, it is service. This message no doubt puzzled the disciples whose world valued honor above all else. It is still a difficult message to hear.

The lawyer in the Samaritan story challenged Jesus by asking what he was supposed to do if he wished eternal life. In this public forum, Jesus had to offer a riposte if he were to maintain honor. Jesus then offered the required counterchallenge by asking the lawyer to describe what the Law said about the question. The challenge-riposte continues as the lawyer challenges Jesus to define "neighbor." After Jesus tells the pointed story of the Samaritan, the lawyer must publicly acknowledge that "the one who treated him with mercy" was the true neighbor. Although the gospel does not record their reaction, the crowd must have admitted that Jesus maintained his honor, since even the lawyer had to concede the point of the story.

Continued Study

There are many other fascinating discoveries for preachers who put on the lenses of social science criticism. As already mentioned, this brief chapter cannot begin to do justice to this or the many other methods of biblical interpretation. The reader will find it helpful to consult *The Social World of Luke-Acts: Models for Interpretation*, already referred to in this chapter. This book is a collection of articles by some of the leading scholars in the field of social science criticism. Preachers who appreciate the need for having an attitude of lifelong learning will certainly immerse themselves in scripture study. The more preachers have a love and knowledge of the scriptures, the more their homilies will be filled with the life found in God's living word.

7. Preaching the Lectionary

Focusing Attention on the Scriptures

The Lectionary has provided an invaluable service in liturgical renewal by allowing the scriptures to reclaim their rightful place as a focal point of worship. Before the reforms of the Second Vatican Council, it was not unusual for preachers to set the scriptures aside so that they could preach a sermon on whatever topic they chose. The liturgy now directs so much attention to the scriptures that it becomes obvious when preachers ignore the prescribed readings. There are, however, some preachers who err on the side of trying to say too much about each of the three readings.

The Lectionary Design

Some preachers feel a need to include all three readings and the responsorial in one homily. Often this involves accommodating the message of the readings as well as some rather creative contortions in homily organization. Those who realize it is not possible to draw a single message from all three readings sometimes end up giving two or three homilies, commenting on each of the readings. Since good homilies have only one central idea, what does a preacher do with all those readings and themes? The design of the Lectionary provides the solution.

The Lectionary is designed to center attention on the gospel. The editors next chose a reading from the Hebrew or Christian scriptures that would complement the theme of the gospel. The middle reading was not chosen with this common link or theme in mind. The middle reading follows Sunday after Sunday on a continual basis. This is true for Sundays in Ordinary Time. On solemnities, all three readings are chosen to reflect the particular celebration. During the seasons of Advent, Lent and Christmas, all readings are chosen according to the theme of the season. What does all this tell the preacher?

Forcing Links

It is often not possible to preach on all three Sunday readings, let alone the responsorial psalm. On the Sundays in Ordinary Time the middle reading will not necessarily reflect the theme or tone of the other two readings. In addition, the gospel and the first reading may have very different messages, although they were chosen to fit together. Editors are not infallible. On some Sundays in Ordinary Time, the first reading may seem at first to reflect the theme of the gospel. The two readings, though, may in fact contain very different messages.

The Fifteenth Sunday in Ordinary Time (Year C) illustrates how the first reading can influence a misreading of the gospel. The first reading is Deuteronomy 30:10-14. Moses tells the people they are to keep God's commandments written in the law and written in their hearts. He tells them they do not need to search distant lands for God's law because "it is something very near to you, already in your mouths and in your hearts; you have only to carry it out" (v. 14). The gospel for that Sunday is the story of the Samaritan.

If the preacher looks for a common link between these two readings, the most obvious single message is that we are to carry out God's law. If we wish to imitate the Samaritan, we are to look into our hearts to find the right thing to do for those in need. This message is true enough. Is that the richest reading of the gospel? Is the Samaritan primarily a model for Christian behavior, or is the Samaritan, in his foolishness, an image of God's unconditional love for people? Although the first reading and the gospel are intended to have the same message, preachers may notice that one of the readings at times forces an interpretation of the other reading.

What about the Second Reading?

Since the second reading does not often parallel the first reading and the gospel, what do preachers do with it? It may be helpful for preachers to think of this reading as the early church reflecting on the experience of what it means to live as a Christian community. In this sense, the reading has an important role in the Liturgy of the Word because it allows the congregation to hear what amounts to a brief homily between the other two readings. If preachers see the second reading in that light, it may often be possible to refer to this reading in the homily, if it does not mean adding a second central idea.

Prayer and Preparation

Careful, scholarly study of the scriptures does not guarantee an effective homily. Lest preachers become mere exegetes in the pulpit, they need to listen to the word in an atmosphere of prayer. *Fulfilled in Your Hearing* (n. 10) reminds us, "There is nothing more essential than prayerful listening for effective preaching, a praying over the texts which seeks the light and fire of the Holy Spirit to kindle the now meaning in our hearts."

Further Reading

Neyrey, Jerome H., ed. *The Social World of Luke-Acts: Models for Interpretation*. Peabody, Mass.: Hendrickson, 1991.

Pazdan, Mary Margaret. "Hermeneutics and Proclaiming the Sunday Readings." *Aquinas Institute of Theology Faculty. In the Company of Preachers*. Collegeville, Minn.: Liturgical Press, 1993, pp. 26-37.

Pontifical Biblical Commission. "The Interpretation of the Bible in the Church." *Origins* 23 (1994): 498-524.

Notes

1. Mary Margaret Pazdan, "Hermeneutics and Proclaiming the Sunday Readings," in *In the Company of Preachers*, ed. Regina Siegfried and Edward Ruane (Collegeville, Minn.: Liturgical Press, 1993), p. 35.

2. Augustine, *On Christian Doctrine,* trans. D. W. Robertson, Jr. (New York: Liberal Arts, 1958), p. 30

3. Charles Bouchard, "Authentic Preaching on Moral Issues," in *In the Company of Preachers*, p. 196.

4. Bouchard, p. 197.

5. Bruce Malina, "Reading Theory Perspective: Reading Luke-

Acts," in *The Social World of Luke-Acts: Models for Interpretation*, ed. Jerome H. Neyrey (Peabody, Mass.: Hendrickson, 1991), p. 16.

6. Pontifical Biblical Commission, "The Interpretation of the Bible in the Church," *Origins* 23 (1994): 498-524.

7. Joseph A. Fitzmyer, *The Biblical Commission's Document "The Interpretation of the Bible in the Church: Text and Commentary"* (Rome: Editrice Pontificio Instituto Biblico, 1995), pp. 26-35.

8. Joseph A. Fitzmyer, "Historical Criticism: Its Role in Biblical Interpretation and Church Life," *Theological Studies* 50 (1989): 248.

9. Sidney Griedanus, *The Modern Preacher and the Ancient Text: Interpreting and Preaching Biblical Literature* (Grand Rapids: Eerdmans, 1988), p. 80.

10. Bruce J. Malina and Richard L. Rohrbaugh, *Social-Science Commentary on the Synoptic Gospels* (Minneapolis: Fortress Press, 1992), p. 11.

11. Malina and Rohrbaugh, p. 71.

12. Douglas E. Oakman, "Was Jesus a Peasant?: Implications for Reading the Samaritan Story (Luke 10:30-35)," *Biblical Theology Bulletin* 22 (1992): 117-25.

13. Oakman, pp. 121-23.

14. Oakman, p. 118.

15. Oakman, p. 120.

16. Oakman, pp. 121-22.

17. Bruce J. Malina and Jerome H. Neyrey, "First-Century Personality: Dyadic, Not Individual," in *The Social World of Luke-Acts: Models for Interpretation*, ed. Jerome H. Neyrey (Peabody, Mass.: Hendrickson, 1991), p. 68.

18. Bruce J. Malina, "Eyes-Heart," in *Biblical Social Values and Their Meanings: A Handbook,* ed. John J. Pilch and Bruce J. Malina (Peabody, Mass.: Hendrickson, 1993), pp. 64-67.

19. Joseph Plevnik, "Honor/Shame," in *Biblical Social Values and Their Meanings: A Handbook,* ed. John J. Pilch and Bruce J. Malina (Peabody, Mass.: Hendrickson, 1993), pp. 95-97.

20. Bruce J. Malina and Jerome H. Neyrey, "Honor and Shame in Luke-Acts: Pivotal Values of the Mediterranean World," in *The Social World of Luke-Acts: Models for Interpretation*, ed. Jerome H. Neyrey (Peabody, Mass.: Hendrickson, 1991), p. 29.

21. Malina and Neyrey, "Honor and Shame in Luke-Acts," pp. 30-31.

Chapter Five

The Preacher's
Own Faith

"You will be my witnesses..." (Acts 1:8)

1. Preaching and Faith

This chapter, more than any other, contains the personal reflections of one preacher speaking with other preachers. I will share more personal experiences here not only as a preacher, but as one who has helped many preachers proclaim their faith. In the introduction to *Preaching: The Art and the Craft*, Walter Burghardt says he will approach the topic not just in terms of research, but from his experience. He goes on to describe how his preaching is more biblical, imaginative and concerned for social justice.[1] His personal tone throughout the book reminds preachers that there is a time for simply talking to one another about what is happening in their ministry.

Do I Believe What I Preach?

Two specific experiences of listening to preachers reflect on their ministry have remained with me for many years. A newly ordained priest was talking about how much he enjoyed preaching in his parish. His words were eloquent and powerful. One Sunday, as he sat for the usual few moments of quiet reflection after the homily, he asked himself, "Do you really believe what you just told these people? Do you live this message?" I need occasionally to challenge myself with the same question. The second experience happened when I was conducting a preaching workshop for clergy. One priest seemed particularly uninterested in the tape of his own homily. I set aside my evaluation sheet and asked him person to person if he could explain why the message seemed so bland. He told me, "Frankly, the people I preach to don't really care about what I have to say." His discouragement emphasized the close connection between faith and enthusiasm for the preaching ministry.

Faith Comes through Hearing

The Letter to the Romans (10:14-15) asks, "But how shall they call on him in whom they have not believed? And how can they believe unless they have heard of him? And how can they hear unless there is someone to preach?" I do not recall where I heard the story about the preacher who quoted that text and preached about how faith must enter through the ears. One little boy in the congregation began to cry near the end of the homily. Outside the church he told the preacher how sad he was because his younger sister was hearing impaired and therefore could not believe in God. I hope the preacher assured the boy that a loving God has ways of allowing his sister to hear the good news. I also hope the preacher did not say that Paul was simply using a figure of speech. Faith does result from preachers who speak the word to listeners who have ears to hear. Martin Luther described the church as a *mouth house*, not a *pen house*.[2]

What Do I Believe about This Word?

As preachers prepare a homily by reading the Lectionary, it is not enough to ask, "What do these readings say?" Just as importantly, preachers must ask, "What do I believe about this word?" When Jesus sent his first disciples forth to preach he promised, "I am with you always, until the end of the age" (Matthew 28:20). As a preacher, do I believe that Jesus is with me in the challenges of my ministry?

At a retreat I attended as a seminarian, the director talked about the many years he enjoyed as a parish minister. He was a gifted preacher with a talent for drawing people into active participation in the liturgy. He especially loved his work with youth. As I listened, I became even more eager to begin ministry. He went on to talk about how he was suddenly asked to leave his lively parish to be the pastor of an inner city congregation. The liturgies at his new parish were poorly attended since there were few Catholics left in the neighborhood. In stark contrast to his earlier success in ministry, he found himself feeling ineffective. Did these people really need him? While he was praying one day in his empty church, he walked up to the tabernacle in which the Eucharist was reserved. Knocking on the tabernacle door, he asked, "God, are you still in there?"

When I was a seminarian preparing for ministry, this story certainly caught my attention. I had to face the possibility that I too might be asked to take on a difficult, lonely assignment. After many years of ministry, I have never needed to knock on a tabernacle door, but I have come close. There have been times when I have had to ask myself whether I really believed Jesus' promise to be with me always.

Preaching As the Integrating Point of Ministry

Ministers study theology, the scriptures, liturgy and pastoral skills. They read newspapers and watch television. They have families and friends. They pray, hope, dream and doubt. All of this knowledge and experience becomes available for others when ministers preach. Preaching—if it comes from within and not merely from a manuscript—is the integrating factor for ministers. It is the moment when an often hectic life suddenly makes sense. Recall Burghardt's observation mentioned in Chapter Three: "From anthropology to zoology, whatever you learn about God's creation is potential grist for your homiletic mill."[3]

Preaching and the Preacher's Identity

Preaching is not merely one more thing that preachers do along with many other ministerial obligations. Because preaching is a matter of one's identity, preachers are always alert to how life experiences can be made available for other believers. Joan Delaplane writes:

> Preaching is not so much a function of one's ministry but an integral dimension of one's identity. To be grounded in the reality "I am a preacher" keeps the focus on the word, not just for proximate preparation to preach but in remote preparation as well.[4]

In homiletics classes and workshops, I ask preachers to critique one another's homilies. They are not to criticize the preacher as a person. This is a healthy group process, but it is not always realistic. Homilies are like fingerprints. A deacon once told me how frightened his elderly pastor was of dying. I asked him if the two men had discussed death. The deacon said, "He never discusses anything serious with me, but I can hear the fear of death in almost every one of his homilies." Fortunately, homiletic fingerprints also help proclaim the good news. I recently attended a parish where a visiting missionary from Thailand was asking for donations for his ministry. I usually find these appeals very trying, especially since in their talks the missionaries pay little attention to the scriptures of the day. This particular young priest, ordained only nine months, did not preach on the readings. However, the obvious love he had for his people, as well as his personal holiness, did preach. Who he was, not what he said in his very broken English, preached eloquently.

Preaching Forms the Preacher

Because authentic preaching relies on the power of God's word, not on human eloquence, preachers are part of the congregation. I find myself often preaching to my own faith journey. Preaching to one's personal needs does not mean homilies are necessarily self-centered. If preachers are personally encouraged and strengthened by the message they have prepared, they can be confident that the homily also speaks to others. John Killinger comments:

> We are formed as we work at giving form to the Word of God. We become more and more like it as we study it and chisel at it and work it into our sermons; until at last, in rhythm with the Word that became flesh, our flesh in a very real sense becomes Word.[5]

Prayer and the Preacher

If preaching is a matter of identity, then preachers must be persons of prayer, not just persons who occasionally pray. Chapter Three stressed the value of preachers asking themselves how the readings specifically link with their lived experience. If preachers enter that process openly, then preparation itself becomes prayer. *Fulfilled in Your Hearing* speaks of this prayerful preparation for preaching. It is not enough that preachers pray before preparation, or alongside their preparation. Prayer is "the very heart and center of the preparation itself" (*Fulfilled*, n. 11). Ministers who prepare homilies in a prayerful atmosphere do so because everything else in their ministry is done in a spirit of prayer. They realize that their ministry is primarily about bringing God and God's people into contact with one another.

Apostolic Prayer

Catholic preachers who daily pray the Liturgy of the Hours or any preachers who regularly pray the psalms have an opportunity to join this prayer with their preaching ministry. Charles E. Miller talks about "Apostolic Prayer" in which the psalms of the Liturgy of the Hours are prayed not just in one's own name, but in the name of specific people among whom preachers minister. Preachers who happen to be very young, for example, may have difficulty identifying with the words in Psalm 71: "Do not cast me aside in my old age; as my strength fails, do not forsake me." Miller suggests that preachers pray these words in the name of the elderly in their congregations.[6] The psalms deal with the whole spectrum of human experience, including illness, betrayal, thanksgiving, joy, loneliness, anger, death and hope. Preachers will certainly identify with some of these emotions and experiences each time they pray the psalms. They will not likely identify with *all* of the psalms, because the psalms cover such a variety of spiritual states. These become opportunities to pray for those in the church who, on their spiritual journey, are perhaps in a different place from the preacher. This type of prayer allows preachers to remain connected with their congregations throughout the week.

Prayer of Confession

Preachers pray in a variety of ways, but there is one type of prayer indispensable for all preachers: the prayer of confession. Although King David was not a preacher, he could come before God, honestly facing and confessing his sins. David is a model for any preacher. While other characters in the scriptures were often hardened by their own faults and sins, David shows a profound sense of humility in his prayers of confession, which set things in their proper perspective. God is Lord, and we people need salvation. Don Saliers points out that facing one's sins is essential for honest preaching: "Proclamation needs such truth-telling to keep the preacher from presumption."[7]

Preachers Are Chosen

Preachers need not become discouraged by their weaknesses if they have the conviction that they have been chosen to proclaim God's word. Just as God did not choose a perfect King David, but a sometimes weak and selfish leader, so God continues to choose ordinary people to bring the good news to God's people. Wallace Fisher discusses this call of ordinary people in the aptly titled book, *Who Dares to Preach?* He offers this encouraging observation:

> So, let the fumblers and the bumblers among us, the slow-witted and the recalcitrant, the weak and the proud—all of us—take heart: biblical preaching is not reserved for an intellectual, moral, or spiritual elite who choose to preach as a favor to God. He chooses, calls, enables and undergirds us...to be his ambassadors, deputies, heralds.[8]

2. Preaching As Witness

In the Footsteps of the First Witnesses

The apostles were teachers, healers and missionaries. Above all, as preachers they were witnesses. When Jesus sent them forth just before the ascension, he promised them, "But you will receive power when the Holy Spirit comes upon you, and you will be my witnesses...to the ends of the earth" (Acts 1:8). In 1 John 1:3 the apostolic author shows an understanding of this mission by concluding, "[W]hat we have seen and heard we proclaim now to you so that you may have fellowship with us...." We who share this apostolic commission to preach are also called to tell others about the Lord we know through our own faith.

Bringing Our Full Selves to Preaching

Writing on evangelization, Paul VI observes, "In the long run, is there any other way of handing on the Gospel than by transmitting to another person one's personal experience of faith?"[9] The chapter on creating homilies mentioned another insight from Paul VI on the importance of personal witness. He concludes that people living in the modern world no longer listen to what teachers have to say unless these teachers also witness what they teach.[10] The consequences for preaching are obvious. It is not enough for preachers merely to teach about God in their homilies. They are called and sent to witness from their personal faith.

Witness involves the risk of allowing others to see God at work in our lives. Writing about the value of preaching the moments of grace in our lives, Frederick Buechner comments on this risk. He notes that there are legitimate reasons to shy away from preaching about these moments of grace. If preachers choose not to preach about them, they still need to "at least preach *out of* them because not to speak from the heart of where your faith comes from is to risk never really touching the hearts of the ones who so hungrily listen."[11]

Witness versus Autobiography

Chapter Two made the point that an outstanding homily requires the word of a witness. That chapter also mentioned that some authorities in homiletics caution preachers never to talk about themselves at the pulpit. I respectfully but strongly disagree with this opinion. In light of what has been said about the identity of the preacher as a person of the word, the apostolic commission to witness to Jesus and the power of witness over teaching, it seems impossible to preach authentically without referring to one's own faith. There is a vast difference between talking about oneself and talking about one's faith in God.

I suspect that those who are adamant about preachers never talking about themselves have heard preachers using *captive therapy*. There is a tendency among some preachers to use the mantle of witness as an excuse to talk out their personal issues from the pulpit. I was visiting a church on the Feast of the Holy Family when the preacher began the homily: "This feast is always difficult for me because I have a paranoid schizophrenic mother and an alcoholic father." I remember nothing else from that homily except feeling sorry for the preacher. He must have had a difficult time growing up. Obviously, experiences from his childhood still influenced his personality. I was not, however, attending to the word of God. This type of captive therapy not only draws attention to the preacher instead of the message, it is a genuine imposition on the congregation. It forces them to listen to the preacher's problems unless they choose to walk out of church. That day I remember several people did leave church. Captive therapy at the pulpit is not always as blatant as this extreme example. It can be subtle. If preachers have doubts about whether a particular witness is appropriate, they can ask themselves, "Will this sharing keep attention on me, or will it allow people to see how God is at work in one person's spiritual journey?"

Witness Nourishes Faith Connections

Preaching from one's personal faith story helps listeners to be more attuned to the ways God may be at work in their lives. Some people think that priests or other celibate preachers must be so otherworldly that they could not possibly understand what real life is all about. When the Sunday readings speak about marriage or other commitments, I like to talk about what it means for me to live as a celibate member of a religious community. I have told people how there were times when I felt "enough is enough!" I have talked about the honeymoon years of priesthood and the years that looked like a divorce was imminent. I am careful to witness that I have persevered not by my will power, but because of a generous God who has confirmed me in my way of life. Without my ever mentioning marriage in the homily, married people understand and identify with this experience. The real issue is not celibacy, nor is it marriage. The preaching issue is that God is the rock on whom any lasting commitment must be built.

Would the homily be as effective if a preacher presented a well-organized, abstract thesis on the importance of commitment and the power of grace? If Paul VI is correct about teachers and witnesses, it seems that abstractions no longer convince. People will listen when they can connect with someone *who has been there*. It is not essential that preachers have the exact life experiences as the congregation. In witness, it is the larger issues underneath the specific experiences that preach. Anger is anger, love is love, belief is belief. When preachers share explicit glimpses of their faith journey, their witness speaks loudly to other believers whose own journey may be down a very different path. The paradox of witness is that when preachers speak in generalities in an attempt to reach the widest possible audience, their message does not connect with the listeners' experiences. The more particular and specific they are in talking about God at work in their own lives, the more people with a variety of experiences will say to themselves, "That preacher knows me well."

Witness and the Preacher's Life

The homily's words are not the only way to witness. A preacher's life must also witness if the preached words are to be credible. In an age when practically no public religious persons are immune from criticism, Mother Theresa of Calcutta enjoyed the universal esteem of believers and nonbelievers alike. Why? How is it that a religious sister who cared for the poor and dying of India received the Nobel Prize for Peace? The world revered this woman because her life offered eloquent testimony of her belief in the dignity of every person. Edward Ruane calls the preacher's personal lived witness, "the acid test of whether the message proclaimed is ideology or genuine praxis."[12]

I have found this connection between preaching and living a life of witness to be one of the more difficult challenges in my years of ministry. Since I am a teacher rather than a parish priest, I often preach in congregations where people do not know me personally. In those settings where I am a visiting priest, my homilies tend to be more courageous in calling people to uncompromising discipleship. It is a different story when I preach back at the seminary or among my brother Vincentians. Those homilies tend to emphasize how God works in broken people. I realize that when I preach about our response to the gospel, at least some people in the congregation will be asking themselves whether they see me as a person striving to live the gospel message. The listeners have a right to ask about my life. Paul VI reminds preachers:

> The world calls for and expects from us simplicity of life, the spirit of prayer, charity towards all, especially towards the lowly and the poor, obedience and humility, detachment and self-sacrifice. Without this mark of holiness, our word will have difficulty in touching the heart of modern man. It risks being vain and sterile.[13]

3. The Language of Faith Experience

Speaking As Believers

On a recent televised celebration of the Eucharist, the preacher began quoting extensively from the *Catechism of the Catholic Church*. The entire homily assumed the tone of instruction. The preacher's message had the authority of the church behind it, but it was not a proclamation of faith. It was an exhortation that we *should have* faith. There was no hint about whether this man had experienced any of the challenges involved in what he was saying. The following homily segments illustrate the difference between the language about faith and the language of lived faith. The first example contains two quotes from the catechism.

Example: Language about Faith

Christ died out of love for us, while we were still "enemies"[Rom. 5:10]. The Lord asks us to love as he does, even our *enemies*, to make ourselves the neighbor of those farthest away, and to love children and the poor as Christ himself (*Catechism of the Catholic Church*, n. 1825).... The practice of all the virtues is animated and inspired by charity...; it is the *form of the virtues*; it articulates and orders them among themselves; it is the source and the goal of their Christian practice. Charity upholds and purifies our human ability to love, and raises it to the supernatural perfection of divine love (*Catechism of the Catholic Church*, n. 1827).

Example: Language of Lived Faith

The other evening I watched a television documentary about World War II veterans. A group of American soldiers traveled to Normandy to relive old memories. It happened that a group of German soldiers was visiting the sight at the same time. Old enemies faced each other. These were men who years before would have been heroes if they had killed each other. Suddenly the former enemies embraced. Not only did they forgive, they wished to become friends. They shared with each other the food they had brought. As I watched that poignant moment I thought of the people whom I might consider enemies. Jesus tells me to forgive them, and in obedience I do, at least halfheartedly. But do I want to embrace them? Do I want to dine with them?

When Faith Meets Experience

Homilies often contain statements of the church's faith. These teachings are not in themselves the language of preaching. To preach on this level is merely to explain what Christians must know and do. All Christians believe, for example, that

- God loves everyone
- Jesus died and rose to save us
- God forgives sinners who repent
- Baptism makes us children of God.

What happens when we ask, "What has been my lived experience?" I believe God loves me. I also know there are times when I have wondered if God even notices some of the difficulties in my life. I have always felt God's forgiveness when I have confessed my sins, but I do wonder what God thinks of my sometimes weak attempts at discipleship. I have also met people who feel God could never forgive them for what they have done. Talking about these experiences is not the language of preaching either. The language of preaching results when preachers allow the faith of the church to interact with their experience of attempting to live this faith. Preaching is neither the abstract language of teachings nor the highly personal language of human doubt and struggle. The following homily is an attempt to link life experiences (mine and the congregation's) with the scriptures.

I preached this homily on the eve of what would have been Martin Luther King, Jr.'s sixty-fifth birthday. At the time, I was fortunate to be helping in a parish that had many simple, generous people who live their discipleship in solid, practical ways. The homily named the grace of discipleship that I saw already active in their lives and mine. It also aimed at encouraging an openness to further service.

The readings were from the Second Sunday in Ordinary Time

(Year B). The gospel (John 1:35-42) was the one in which John the Baptist points out Jesus as the lamb of God. The first disciples follow to see where Jesus stays. The first reading was 1 Samuel 3:3-10,19, describing the Lord waking young Samuel three times as he slept in the temple. Eli at last tells Samuel to say, "Speak, Lord, for your servant is listening."

In this sample homily, as in the homily in Chapter Four, the phrases in brackets at the start of each section provide indications of the development of the homily.

Sample Homily: Come and See

[Civil Rights and a Sleeping Church] Tomorrow our nation celebrates the sixty-fifth birthday of Dr. Martin Luther King, Jr. We remember not just the birthday of an important person, but also celebrate his famous dream. Dr. King had a dream that all God's children would one day be treated with the dignity they deserve, despite differences such as the color of their skin or their religion. People have dignity because they are God's children. Dr. King spoke of this dream at a time when many people in our country were asleep. Some political candidates of the time, especially in the South, would give speeches with one finger held up while they would arrogantly proclaim, "not one!" The crowd knew this meant: "Not one black child would be admitted to the all-white public schools." And the crowds cheered. We might wonder how Christian people could act like that. Too many people were asleep, choosing not to notice what was going on. I mention this not just because of the holiday tomorrow, but also to help us appreciate the situation going on in our first reading, from the Book of Samuel.

[Samuel Is Awakened] The first reading today, in which Samuel is awakened three times, tells us that God's followers were not attentive to God's voice. Many of the supposedly religious people at this time in history were not all that different from the kind of person in Martin Luther King, Jr.'s time who chose not to notice how minorities were being treated. Or if they did notice, they felt it had nothing to do with their religion. Just as too many Christian people were apathetic about discrimination, many people in these ancient times of Samuel were apathetic about following their God, Yahweh.

Our reading says that young Samuel is asleep in the Temple. He was supposed to be awake. It was his job to keep the sacred Temple lamp burning—a sign of God's presence. But many believers were asleep in terms of living their faith. The reading says Samuel could not recognize God's voice, probably because the people had made a practice of not being attentive to God's voice. They had gradually learned to shut God out of their lives. Old Eli remembers enough of the good old faithful days to offer the right advice. He tells young Samuel, "If you hear the voice again, say, 'Speak, Lord, your servant is listening.'" As Samuel at last opens himself up to God's voice, God begins a new era among the people. It is the start of a renewed relationship between God and the believers, an era when, among other leaders, God raises up King David. The voice of God that starts this renewed relationship is repeated much later in time when the voice of Jesus calls out to his followers. That is what we hear in the gospel today.

[Jesus Continues the Call] When Jesus appears at the start of John's gospel, not everyone was alert enough to hear his voice or recognize him as the one sent from God. Evidently God's people were asleep once again. But John the Baptist could recognize Jesus' voice. Andrew and his unnamed companion could recognize Jesus' voice. They immediately began to follow Jesus. We have a wonderful scene here where the first two disciples are tagging along behind Jesus and he suddenly turns around and says, "What are you looking for?" They answer that they want to know where Jesus is staying. Jesus invites them to find out: "Come, and you will see."

When Jesus says, "Come, and you will see," he is doing far more than simply offering a tour of his lodgings. He is inviting the disciples to *really see*—to open their eyes and have a good look at him, to see that he is their Lord. When the gospels tell us Jesus cured blind people, those stories are not just about healed retinas and corneas. God is reaching into people's lives and inviting them to take a good hard look, to really see the Lord and hear his voice, to become followers.

[Jesus Calls Us to Follow] This is a special gospel for me because it was read the first day I entered the seminary. In those days after grace was said at meals we all sat in silence and listened to a scripture passage. Most of us had just left home, said goodbye to our families and were in this strange new place. The student doing the reading chose this gospel. I remember clearly feeling like the disciples as Jesus told them to come and see where he lived. Come and stay with me. For a long time I felt the only way to stay with Jesus as a disciple was to live apart from the world and all its activity. I would need to be in constant silence, spending most of the day in prayer. That would be the real way to come and see where Jesus is, I thought. A life of quiet prayer and work is the way Jesus calls monks and cloistered nuns to follow him. That must be their way. It is not true for most of us. Jesus' invitation to the disciples today is also given to each of us right where we are in life. Jesus calls us to follow him not by stepping out of our daily lives, but by stepping more fully into our daily lives. Whether we are priests or religious or married or single, wherever the Lord has found us, we are to follow as disciples.

[Discipleship in This Parish] I have been profoundly edified by the many ways I see people in this parish respond to Jesus' call to follow. I see people being disciples by helping in the food pantry. I see people bringing the Eucharist to shut-ins. When I presided at a recent parish funeral, I was impressed by the way people here prepared a meal for the family and friends who attended the funeral. It's dangerous to start naming ways people live discipleship because there are so many quiet, unnoticed ways folks follow the Lord behind the scenes. This is true for those who give so much personal energy to family members, or to sick friends or to people with whom they work. Sometimes all of this service can become challenging and tiresome. Maybe we sometimes wonder if it all matters. It does. It is the concrete way we respond to Jesus when he invites us to come see where he lives. That effort is the way we live our discipleship. It is our personal way of saying, along with Samuel, "Speak, Lord, your servant is listening."

[Disciples Want to Share What They Find] Notice in this gospel that the first disciples did not just go off and follow Jesus as a private matter between the Lord and them. Andrew thinks about his brother Simon. He runs off to tell him about the wonderful new teacher they have found. He invites Simon to share in the life of discipleship. Are we like Andrew? Do we invite others along to follow the Lord? Andrew found Jesus and could hardly wait to invite his brother along to discover the Lord also. How about us? Can people look at us and see that the Lord has made a difference to us? Do they want to come along and see the person we have found?

[In This Eucharist Jesus Invites Us to Come] On the night before he died, Jesus gathered at supper with Andrew, Simon and the other early followers. He chose a way to allow them to be with him always through the breaking of bread. You and I are invited to that same experience of the Lord today at this table. Here, we can come and see where the Lord lives. We must not keep the experience in this church. As we return to our families, our work, our play and all the other daily activities of our lives, may we bring the Lord with us. May we show others, by the way we treat them, that we have found someone special and would like them also to know the Lord.

4. Discovering the God We Preach

Homilies reveal the personal faith of the speaker, whether or not preachers intend to talk explicitly about their faith. Even if preachers attempt to bury their faith in theological abstractions, something of their personal beliefs and doubts comes through. Chapter Six, "Listening to the Listeners," includes a strategy for finding out what congregations hear about the preacher's own faith. The final part of this chapter looks at what preachers intend to say and have others hear about God.

A Preacher's Image of God

The Bible reveals a God who has many faces. Genesis describes a powerful creator who enjoys evening walks in the garden with Adam. Many prophets speak in the name of a God who is offended at the oppression of the poor and the powerless. Hosea describes God as a gentle parent who teaches children to walk. This God warmly hugs these children. Few people are mindful of this rich variety of revelation when they pray or preach. Most of us are comfortable with one primary image of God. This is the God who permeates our preaching. In my own experience, my image of God shifts periodically, depending upon how God happens to be working in my life at a particular time.

God As Creator

I see God as creator when I spend time with young families. In a parish where I used to minister, I enjoyed watching a young married couple beaming when they told me they were expecting their first child. They always sat close to one another in their customary front pew, but it seemed to me they sat even closer as the birth of the first child grew nearer. When I spend time with young families, my homilies often feature God, the creator of new life.

God As Infinite

I have lived mostly in very noisy, crowded neighborhoods that have afforded little occasion to think of vast open spaces. I seldom think of God as infinite. A few years ago I was delighted to spend several months working in Florida. I went to the beach as often as I could. As I waded in waters that stretched from where I stood to the shores of Ireland and England, God became very large, infinite. I could hear this limitlessness of God in my preaching.

God As Unconditional Lover

My fourth-grade teacher was 106 years old when she died. I loved to visit this Sister of Loretto mainly because I could walk on water in her presence. Her face would light up and her arms reach out for a big hug when I entered her room. She admitted that I might have a fault or two, but those only made me more interesting and fully human in her eyes. I seldom have difficulty seeing the face of God as one who unconditionally loves me: I just picture my very special friend. If I preached shortly after visiting her, the congregation heard from a God who loves us with no strings attached.

Preaching the Whole God

God has other faces besides these three I especially enjoy. God is redeemer, healer, liberator, champion of the poor, gentle father and mother, spiritual guide, good friend. The face of God with whom individuals are most at peace may not be the face of God revealed in the scriptures for a particular liturgy. We preach the faith of the church, not private spirituality. Ministry may demand that we expand our image of God so that we do not impose a narrow interpretation on the scriptures we are called to proclaim.

In Matthew 5:1-12, Jesus preaches the beatitudes that turn our comfortable lives upside down. Suddenly, they are blessed who are poor in spirit, sorrowing, lowly and persecuted. Jesus shows a face of God who loves the poor. For the comfortable, this is not a comfortable image of God. One priest preached these beatitudes as "helpful hints for happiness." He brought his image of God to the scriptures rather than allowing the scriptures to show him the face of God. The issue is even more obvious when Matthew's Sermon on the Mount is contrasted with Luke's sermon "on the level stretch" (Luke 6:17-27). In Luke, Jesus does not simply side with the poor *in spirit*, but with the materially poor and hungry. Furthermore, Jesus goes on to add a series of woes toward the rich and well fed. Philip Van Linden concludes that Luke's audience probably parallels the church in the United States, made up of the rich, the poor and those between these extremes. Jesus calls people from all economic levels to be detached from materialism and to love the poor.[14] God is certainly doing more than offering a few helpful hints for happiness.

Exegeting Past Homilies

Just as preachers carefully study the scriptures to discover what God is revealing in the word, we can also exegete our past homilies to discover the face of God we are preaching. I have copies of nearly every homily I have preached. I doubt they will ever be used to support my future cause for sainthood, but they do offer me an excellent opportunity to see the face of God I have preached at various times in my life. My earliest homilies would have made Pelagius very proud. I suspect as a young priest I must have had a strong messiah complex because I had better advice for people than the scriptures offered. These manuscripts are an interesting record of how the face of God has mellowed over the years. God is now more patient. God has a much healthier sense of humor, too.

God in Our Personal Salvation History

The scriptures tell the story of *the* salvation history through which God saves us in a series of events. From the creation of a peaceful garden out of the chaos of churning waters, to the otherworldly visions found in Revelation, God has been busy in human history. Someone once observed that every individual recapitulates this salvation history. Each of us has experiences of creation, the Exodus, the cross and resurrection. I still remember the sense of awe with which one of my brothers described the birth of his first son. He saw the creator at work. God brought a captive people out of Egyptian slavery. God continues to bring people out of the bondage of chemical dependencies and crippling emotional fears. In the sacrament of reconciliation each of us has firsthand experience of the victory involved in the cross and resurrection. Our salvation histories are filled with people and events that God has used to form us into God's own people.

Since homilies link the lives of the faithful to God's word in the scriptures, preachers need to be in touch with the saving moments in their lives. A retreat director once suggested that I spend time writing down all the important events and people in my life, starting with my first significant memory. At this stage, he said, it is not necessary to be thinking of God or salvation history—just list the history. Later, I went over the list and looked for hints of God's hand at work. None of these events will ever provide material for great books or films, but they were the ways God has been active in my personal salvation history. Being aware of these saving moments helps preachers see that the great stories of scripture continue in their own lives and the lives of those among whom they preach.

A Challenge to Preachers

During my first year of priesthood, I lived at a high school seminary while continuing graduate studies. At the opening Mass for the new school year, the chapel was filled with young men eager to be priests one day. The faculty was gathered in the sanctuary, concelebrating this festive liturgy. One of my favorite people, Father Victor, stepped into the pulpit. He removed his Ben Franklin-style reading glasses. In his best dramatic voice he told the bright-eyed students, "Young men, go home!" There was a gasp from my fellow concelebrants. "I say it again, go home! Go home unless you are willing to give your entire lives to what you are supposed to be about." He continued with a magnificent homily filled with gospel challenge. The homily showed a deep appreciation for what Jesus asked of his first preachers in the gospel according to Luke.

Three Rebuffs for Preachers

In Luke 9:57-62, three would-be disciples announce their desire to follow Jesus. Jesus confronts each with surprising challenges. Robert Karris offers an interpretation of these rebuffs as uncompromising challenges to discipleship.[15] The first agrees to follow Jesus "wherever you go." Jesus responds by saying that even the foxes and birds have a home, "but the Son of Man has nowhere to rest his head." Disciples who wish to preach cannot be overly concerned with their own comfort. The second person agrees to follow Jesus provided he can first bury his dead father. Jesus responds, "Let the dead bury their dead. But you, go and proclaim the kingdom of God." Preaching the kingdom is about life, not death. The spiritually dead can take care of burying the physically dead. There can be no more "business as usual" for those who preach the word. Third, a potential disciple asks to return home to say goodbye to his people. Jesus says that once the hand is put to the plow there is no looking back. Good farmers know they must keep looking ahead for straight furrows. If they keep looking back, there will be very crooked rows. The kingdom calls for preachers who have energy and determination.

The Preacher's Faith

Before I entered the seminary, I met someone I think about nearly every time I reflect on the link between preaching and one's own faith. Two weeks before quitting my job I began telling clients that I was leaving work so I could go back to school. My clients were from Chicago's skid row. I worked in the office of a company that hired people as day laborers. A man I will call Tom waited around in our office after he and the other men had received their daily paychecks. He told me that he heard I was leaving to become a priest. He told me in a very serious tone of voice that he hoped the ministry would be better to me than it had been to him. That got my attention. He told me about the time he had been a pastor in a small town parish. He had a wonderful wife and three children. Life was good. One evening he came home to find a state police officer waiting on his front porch. The police officer had the terrible news that the pastor's wife and children had been killed in an auto accident. Tom told me, "I walked away from my church that night, and I will never set foot in a church again. I simply do not believe there can be a God who would let something like that happen to my family."

I still wonder what happened to Tom. I wonder if he and God ever made peace with each other. I do not judge him. Who knows how any of us would react to such a sudden, awful tragedy as he was asked to face? I do question how much he had preached out of his own faith. Had he preached the whole story from the scriptures? Had he preached a discipleship that involves the cross, not in the abstract, but in terms of his lived experience? When I think about it, I say a prayer for Tom. I hope all of us will pray for one another as we try to faithfully preach the God in whom we believe.

Further Reading

Burghardt, Walter J. "What Shall a Man Give in Exchange?" in *Preaching: The Art and the Craft*. New York: Paulist Press, 1987, pp. 173-91.

Miller, Charles E. "Prayer and the Homilist." *The Priest* 46 (October 1990): 9-10.

Notes

1. Walter J. Burghardt, *Preaching: The Art and the Craft* (New York:

Paulist Press, 1987), p. 2.

2. Fred W. Meuser and Stanley D. Schneider, eds., *Interpreting Luther's Legacy* (Minneapolis: Augsburg, 1969), p. 30.

3. Walter J. Burghardt, "From Study to Proclamation," in *A New Look at Preaching*, ed. John Burke (Wilmington, Del.: Michael Glazier, 1983), p. 27.

4. Joan Delaplane, "Spirituality of the Preacher," in *Concise Encyclopedia of Preaching*, ed. William H. Willimon and Richard Lischer (Louisville: Westminster/Knox, 1995), p. 448.

5. John Killinger, *The Centrality of Preaching in the Total Task of the Ministry* (Waco, Tex.: Word, 1969), p. 35.

6. Charles E. Miller, *Ordained to Preach: A Theology and Practice of Preaching* (New York: Alba House, 1992), pp. 21-23.

7. Don Saliers, "Prayer," in *Concise Encyclopedia of Preaching*, ed. William H. Willimon and Richard Lischer (Louisville: Westminster/Knox, 1995), p. 378.

8. Wallace E. Fisher, *Who Dares to Preach?: The Challenge of Biblical Preaching* (Minneapolis: Augsburg, 1979), p. 78.

9. Paul VI, *On Evangelization in the Modern World (Evangelii Nuntiandi)* (December 8, 1975), n. 46.

10. Paul VI, Address to the Members of the Consilium de Laicis (October 2, 1974) *Acta Apostolicae Sedis* 66 (1974): 568.

11. Frederick Buechner, "By Grace We Are Saved," *The Living Pulpit* 4.1 (1995): 5.

12. Edward Ruane, "The Spirituality of a Preacher," Aquinas Institute of Theology Faculty, in *In the Company of Preachers*, ed. Regina Siegfried and Edward Ruane (Collegeville, Minn.: Liturgical Press, 1993), p. 158.

13. Paul VI, *On Evangelization in the Modern World*, n. 76.

14. Philip Van Linden, *The Gospel of Luke and Acts* (Wilmington, Del.: Michael Glazier, 1986), p. 81.

15. Robert J. Karris, "The Gospel According to Luke," in *The New Jerome Biblical Commentary*, ed. Raymond E. Brown, Joseph A. Fitzmyer, and Roland E. Murphy, (Englewood Cliffs, N.J.: Prentice Hall, 1990), p. 701.

Chapter Six

Listening to the Listeners

How Do Preachers Include Other Voices?

1. Preaching Belongs to the Church

Preachers frequently use the expression "I need to work on my homily." In the sense that preachers devote study, prayer and work to preaching, the homily is uniquely the preacher's. There is also a sense in which a homily belongs to the entire church, not just to individual preachers. This chapter deals with including many voices in the homily. The Second Vatican Council reminds us: "The faithful indeed, by virtue of their royal priesthood, participate in the offering of the Eucharist" (*Dogmatic Constitution on the Church*, n. 10).

Preaching matters to listeners. Mention the topic of preaching to a group of people, and everyone has comments to contribute. Some people remark that good preaching is one of the most important needs in the church. Others relate "horror stories" concerning bad homilies to which they have been subjected. These latter individuals often have a collection of jokes about preaching. Even these negative reactions reveal a hunger for good preaching, according to David Schlafer: "For why, after all, would people continue to criticize what they really do not care about?"[1] Whether the faithful praise preaching, joke about bad preaching or merely endure it, they do care.

Revisiting the Definition of a Homily

Chapter One defined a homily in terms of its effect on the hearers. A homily is not a finished product that preachers hand over to passive listeners. Preachers and listeners together meet the person of Christ. Schlafer suggests the metaphor of a photographic "positive" and "negative" in considering this interactive dimension of preaching. A finished photo (the positive) is a fixed image. Some preachers consider their finely polished homilies in this static sense. A photographic negative, on the other hand, appears more fluid, bearing little resemblance to the print. In a real sense the negative is the opposite of the finished print. Without this negative, however, there could be no picture. Schlafer observes that preaching is like the negative in that all the elements are there to produce an effect in the listeners. The interaction of these elements, not the static homily text, is the basis for good preaching.[2] Note that this definition of a homily essentially describes what it achieves, not what it looks or sounds like:

> A homily is a preaching event that is integral to the liturgy to proclaim the saving mystery of God in the scriptures. It calls and empowers the hearers to faith, a deeper participation in the Eucharist, and daily discipleship to Christ lived out in the church.

The Test of Good Preaching

This definition has significant consequences for the listeners and for the preachers, who are also listeners to God's word. The true test of good preaching is the effect it produces in the lives of believers. Although good preaching involves prayer, research and careful crafting, none of these activities guarantees an effective homily. Here are seven characteristics that separate authentic liturgical preaching from all other forms of communication.

A. Preaching is the work of the Spirit within listeners as well as preachers.

Models of the communication process illustrate how a carefully crafted message will produce the speaker's desired effect in the audience. Highly skilled speakers learn techniques for achieving their purposes. Preaching involves an added variable in the communication process. Ultimately, the effectiveness of the preached word does not rest with the preachers' skills. The Spirit of God at work in preachers and listeners makes a homily effective. "God's Word does what God wills, not what the preacher wills."[3] The Spirit who is at work in the preacher is the same Spirit who is at work in the listeners. This means that preachers need to be receptive to the movements of the Spirit in those who hear the preaching.[4]

Some preachers have appealed to the Spirit's role in preaching as an excuse to avoid preparing homilies. Effective preachers realize that they bring the same level of expertise to the pulpit that other communicators exercise in their professions. The Holy Spirit does not supplant the hard work of writing a homily. The Spirit makes a preacher's words effective in the listener. Paul VI describes the Spirit as the "soul of the Church" who possesses the evangelizers and the listeners (*On Evangelization in the Modern World*, n. 56).

B. Preaching is an event of grace.

Since the Spirit is the source of efficacy in preaching, homilies are not merely rhetorical events; they are events of grace. Vincent de Paul recounts an incident that describes how the community of priests and brothers that he founded was the result of grace at work in preaching. In 1617, at the prompting of Madame de Gondi, a pious lady in Folleville, France, Vincent preached a sermon on the importance of making a general confession of one's past life. As a result of his preaching, a huge crowd came to confession, and Madame de Gondi had to send for more priests. Vincent told the priests and brothers of his congregation that he had never intended to found a religious congregation. The effects surrounding the Folleville sermon were not the fruits of human strategy, but the work of grace.[5] Karl Rahner describes preaching as a "salvific event" that "renders the grace of God present."[6] The word of God is the *dabar* that has its own dynamism and power to produce effects in the hearers.[7]

C. Preaching names the grace already at work in the listeners.

Although this book's definition of a homily stresses that preaching is an event of grace, this does not imply that homilies introduce God into a nonbelieving congregation. As Catherine Hilkert argues in her book *Naming Grace*, preaching identifies God's activity already at work within the congregation. One's theology of preaching depends on one's theology of revelation. If revelation is God speaking from beyond our world, then preaching becomes a process of repeating the biblical stories in the hope that they will speak to people today. If, on the other hand, revelation is open and ongoing in the depths of human experience, then preachers name grace already at work among the people. Preaching names the grace in terms of images found in the scriptures and tradition.[8] *Fulfilled in Your Hearing* (n. 20) also speaks of preaching as a process of naming grace. Preachers do not "so much attempt to explain the Scriptures as to interpret the human situation through the Scriptures."

D. Preaching is about faith *in* Christ, not only knowledge *about* Christ.

Do homilies merely explain who Christ is, or do they bring Christ and believers into personal contact? Roman Catholic documents reflect a tension between preaching that teaches about Christ and preaching that proclaims the person of Christ in the midst of believers. Martin Luther characterized this tension in terms of *law and gospel*. Chapter Seven describes Luther's insight in more detail.

Steven DeLeers notes that the modern debate over explanation and proclamation began at the Second Vatican Council. *The Constitution on the Sacred Liturgy* contains both emphases. DeLeers concludes that the 1981 document, *De verbo Dei*, eases the tension between explanation and proclamation. The document states that even when homilies teach, they must lead the community to faith expressed by participation at the liturgy. Homilies never simply explain.[9]

The Catechism of the Catholic Church again raises the question of homilies that teach, more than proclaim, the person of Christ. Some preachers use the catechism—not the Lectionary—as a source for homilies. Homilies are not about information, but about faith.

E. Preaching often leads to surprising results.

Good preachers prepare homilies aimed at specific responses. A homily is not necessarily a failure if the congregation cannot voice a response that corresponds with the preacher's intended aim. Preaching is an invitation, not a command. Other types of communication, for instance, advertising or political speeches, usually aim at achieving one specific goal: persuading people to buy the advertised product or to vote for the "right" candidate. Preaching produces a multiplicity of responses. Believers bring a variety of needs to the preaching moment. The preached word often speaks on many levels to different believers. Preachers can neither predict nor control how believers will respond to the word. "The wind blows where it wills…; so it is with everyone who is born of the Spirit" (John 3:8).

F. Preaching embodies the power to change, not the command that people should change.

Chapter Seven, "Preaching the Prophetic Word," deals with the difference between homilies that merely tell people they should change, and homilies that preach Christ who is the power to change. Simply telling people what God expects of them is no substitute for preaching the person and power of Christ. In the Acts of the Apostles, for example, preaching led listeners to personal conversion. The author of Acts says that people soon spoke of the newly converted as Christians. Raymond Brown considers this early apostolic preaching to be a fitting paradigm for the contemporary church. While not ignoring the fact that there are behavioral consequences to Christianity, the essence of the message is still the person of God acting in Jesus Christ.[10]

G. Preaching links the human story with God's story.

Roger Van Harn's *Pew Rights: For People Who Listen to Sermons* lists ten preaching "rights" that congregations have as members of the church. The first of these rights states, "When we listen to sermons, *we have a right to hear a Word addressed to our deepest needs.*"[11] Homilies that respect the listeners' deepest needs avoid the trivial and the irrelevant. Authentic preaching bridges the artificial gap we create between the world of human experience and God's world. John Shea believes that preachers waste energy by contriving illustrations and images that explain God's world as if it were somehow apart from our human world.[12]

Karl Rahner equates the preacher with a poet who uses *primordial words* "which spring from the heart, which hold us in their power, which enchant us, the glorifying, heaven-sent words."[13] Preaching on this level goes beyond attempts to explain the human situation or the ways of God. When preachers delve into the depths of life experience and the mystery of the scriptures, they proclaim a healing word that links the listeners' deepest needs with the good news that is the word of life.

2. Exegeting the Congregation

The World of the Congregation

Conscientious preachers invest a great deal of energy exegeting the scriptures as an integral step in preparing homilies. Exegesis of the readings is only part of the preparation process. Preachers must also exegete the congregation by asking, "Who will listen to this message?" Exegesis of the listeners—seeking to understand them, their education, ethnicity and the like—allows preachers "to speak both for and to a congregation."[14] As mentioned earlier, it is important for preachers to write homilies that preach to their own faith needs. If a homily is good news for the preacher, it is likely to be good news for the congregation. However, if preachers reflect only on their own world of faith experience, the homily will likely exclude other voices in the community. Various methods of exegeting the scriptures offer direction for exegeting the congregation. The social science method discussed in Chapter Four, for example, asks questions of the scripture text concerning the world of the author and first listeners.

The following list of categories offers a brief, general glimpse of the congregation's world. It is not intended to be an exhaustive tool for analysis, but merely suggests ways preachers can begin to exegete the congregation.

Age

Young families are concerned about raising their children in the faith, the quality of their married and family life and providing for the future. The young are very invested in the present and the future of this world. They look to homilies that will help them find meaning in their ever-changing lives. The elderly have dealt with these issues throughout their lives. They are now looking for a hopeful word that will strengthen them as they begin to face death. Preaching can help them let go of their lives in anticipation of the life to come.

Ethnicity

Different cultures and ethnic groups have their own religious symbols, stories and traditions. Many Native American nations refer to God as "Grandfather." Many African Americans are at home in a world familiar with stories from the Bible and songs of liberation from oppression. Spanish-speaking Christians are too often lumped together in one ethnic group. In fact, people from Cuba, Mexico, Latin America, Puerto Rico and many other lands express their faith in a variety of ways. Preachers must listen carefully to the faith stories of these groups.

Education

In many communication settings, the education level of a target audience is a crucial factor in shaping the message. Lawyers, for example, will conduct extensive interviews with potential jury members to decide what types of appeals will be most persuasive in presenting their case. While this factor cannot be ignored in preaching, it is often difficult to shape a homily in light of the educational level of the congregation, because typical congregations are composed of people with a wide variety of educational experience. In addition, a homily is a unique type of communication whose power does not lie in wise argumentation or clever discourse, but on the Spirit (1 Corinthians 2:4).

Income

Chapter Four affirmed that the income level of the listeners influenced the way they heard the parable of the "Good Samaritan." The peasants in Jesus' audience considered the wealthy, and therefore untrustworthy, Samaritan to be foolish for getting involved in the problems of the man beaten by robbers. Most congregations have their materially poor, their wealthy and many people who fall between these extremes. Does income level influence how homilies are heard today?

Neighborhood

Some Catholic congregations are composed of people who all live in the same neighborhood. In larger cities with many churches, the congregation may live within a very limited area. One parish took advantage of this situation by organizing a weekly "witness walk" in which a group of parishioners walked through their changing neighborhood, picking up trash from the streets. Curious unchurched neighbors asked them who they were and what they were doing. This became an opportunity to invite neighbors to the parish. This parish adopted a mission statement in which members described themselves as a leaven of stability in their changing neighborhood. Preachers in parishes with this type of commitment to the neighborhood can appeal to this common experience in linking the lives of the congregation to the scriptures.

Faith Experience

The most important area of congregational exegesis involves listening to the ways people describe their faith experiences. Homily discussion groups, for instance, can provide insights that help preachers appreciate how the word affects people's lives. When a preacher, to use an example, uses these words of Jesus in a homily, "No one can serve two masters....You cannot serve God and mammon" (Matthew 6:24), what does that challenge mean to various people in the congregation? A single mother on welfare will hear those words differently than a wealthy business person. A seminarian remarked that those words played an important part in his decision to leave his successful investment firm so that he could pursue the priesthood. Preachers will enliven their homilies when they include these rich faith experiences of their listeners.

What Listeners and Preachers Share

Despite the variety of faith stories in every worshipping community, preachers and listeners do share common faith experiences. Celibate Roman Catholic priests and men and women religious share a great deal with married couples, for example, in the sense that their different life choices all involve permanent commitment. This commitment is lived out in unique ways, but priests and religious, as well as married laity, deal with fidelity, times of disillusion, the tedium of routine and the sometimes nagging questions about whether one has made the right choice. David Buttrick examines some of these religious constants in "Who Is Listening?"[15] Preachers can more easily touch the deepest longings and needs of listeners when they become more aware of how much their own religious experiences have in common with those of the people in their congregations. Before considering these common faith experiences, it may be helpful to add that preachers and listeners often articulate their faith differently.

Some preachers may consider themselves more religious than their congregations. They believe their homilies bring religion into the lives of the laity living in a secular age. Buttrick reminds preachers that their people are already generally religious. The laity may have difficulty articulating their faith lives since "religion is tangled up with the total mix of their humanity."[16] Preachers have the theological vocabulary to talk about God's unconditional love, but parents know what it means to stay up all night with a sick child without thinking they are doing anything special, and an elderly husband knows about living with his wife who has Alzheimer's disease. Preachers may appeal to the congregation's need to create Christian community, but teenagers know what it means to invite an unpopular boy or girl to join them, knowing "it is a good thing to do." God is active in the lives of people even though they may not be able to articulate that grace in theological terms. Preachers do not introduce the notion of religion to a nonreligious people. This is further support of Catherine Hilkert's insight that preaching names the grace already present in the community.[17]

Self-Justification

The first common faith experience, or religious constant, that preachers and listeners share is a "profound inner alienation" that is rooted in the tension between the persons we see ourselves to be, and the persons others tell us we are by the way they treat us. Most of us attempt to ease this tension by strategies that seek the approval of others. Buttrick observes, "If others admire us, or even like us, why, then, perhaps we can approve [of] ourselves."[18] Advertisers appeal to this inner alienation by images that promise we will be healthier, happier, wealthier and more popular if we use their products. When Jesus had the poor taste to dine in the home of Levi, the tax collector, some questioned his disciples about why they mingled with that unacceptable element of society. Jesus responded, "I have not come to call the righteous to repentance but sinners" (Luke 5:32). The gospel frees preachers and listeners from the need to justify themselves. Homilies announce the refreshing good news that people do not have to make themselves worthy of God's love. We are already worthy because God loves us first.

Inner Oughts

The second constant that Buttrick says preachers share with listeners is the tendency to impose inner "oughts" on themselves. We internalize more guilt than we do God's unearned grace.[19] This is not to say guilt has no place in modern religious experience. It is rather a question of getting things out of balance. Preaching is not about adding countless demands on ourselves. It is about proclaiming Jesus who is the power by which we can live as his disciples. Preachers and listeners may be comfortable with moralistic homilies that merely tell us what we should and should not do. That type of preaching gives us the illusion of control over our faith lives. Preaching Jesus as the one who freely gives salvation takes away the burden of trying to save ourselves, but it also takes away much of the control we think we have.

Loneliness

A third common faith experience that most people share is a certain level of loneliness. Even if we interact with people throughout the day, there is still a mysterious dimension to others that we never really touch. Most of us never fully touch the mysterious center within ourselves.[20] This common experience that preachers and listeners have in common offers preachers a powerful opportunity to proclaim a God who does know our secret recesses. "More tortuous than all else is the human heart, beyond remedy; who can understand it? I, the Lord, alone probe the mind and test the heart..." (Jeremiah 17:9-10).

Need for Meaning

In describing the fourth constant, Buttrick reminds preachers that most of us experience a sense that we were born for a purpose.[21] Preachers and listeners share a craving for meaning in a world that increasingly devalues individual humans. Abortion and euthanasia offer dramatic examples. There are also more subtle experiences that daily cloud our sense of being a person with purpose and meaning. An army recruit once related how the men and women at his boot camp would crowd into the small chapel every Sunday. "It was a sacred place and time for me. This was the only place I could go where my superiors could not tell me what to do." Sunday worship may be one of the few opportunities many people have to step out of a depersonalized world to reflect on their meaning and purpose as God's family.

Preaching As Connection

This chapter began by stating that preaching is not the sole property of preachers. It belongs to the entire church. Homilies connect preachers with listeners, and listeners with one another. The chapter to this point has attempted to show how these many voices support the preacher's one voice. The rest of the chapter offers practical models for helping preachers and listeners connect with one another so that many voices preach.

3. Listening before Homilies

Preachers can benefit by listening to the listeners both before and after they preach homilies. Before homilies are preached, listeners can add their voices to preaching by sharing instances of their own faith experience. This section offers several models for listening to the listeners who add their voices as the homily takes shape.

The Word of a Witness

Some homiletics authorities, discussed in Chapter Five, advise preachers never to talk about themselves in homilies. They are concerned that preachers who tell their own story run the risk of focusing the message on themselves, not on the word of God. There is a difference between personal stories that focus on the preacher, and stories that witness God's moves in one person's life. Authentic personal witness is one of the most effective ways to preach the gospel, as the apostle Paul knew well. However, preachers need not limit witness to their own faith story. Homilies proclaim the faith of the entire church. How can preachers bring these other voices into the pulpit?

Seeing God in Life Experience

Some preachers take refuge in ecclesiastical language when they speak about God. They can quote the Bible, church documents and catechisms with flawless precision. They fail, though, to see that God also speaks through human experiences. This is a risky area. Preaching possesses the authority of the church when it remains in the language of official documents, and it enjoys the authority of God's word when it speaks in the language of the Bible, but when preaching speaks about God at work in the lives and events around us, it becomes open to objections. How can we be sure a particular person or event shows us the hand of God? The ambiguity of religious experience is not a new problem.

God tried three times to get the attention of young Samuel sleeping in the Temple. Not until an aged Eli finally discerned that God was at work was he able to advise Samuel to listen for God's voice (1 Samuel 3:1-11). God continues to speak through people and events, and it is still usually difficult to hear God's voice in the midst of life's noise. This is not to suggest that preaching deals with private revelations. Some television evangelists have proclaimed, "God has given me a message and asked me to speak to you this morning." God is free to make private revelations to individuals, but the common experience of the church has been that God works in more subtle movements. Parents of newborn children can see the hand of God continuing the work of Genesis as new life is created. Persons freed from chemical dependencies have an experience of Exodus deliverance. Business people struggling with difficult ethical decisions may experience a Jesus who was tempted as we are. Preachers and congregations who find themselves renewed by a powerful homily have a glimpse of an ongoing Pentecost. If preachers and listeners approach their everyday lives as believers looking for the hand of God, they will find the Lord in their midst. Where can preachers and listeners share these stories?

Homily Discussion Groups

The first step in bringing other voices into the pulpit involves listening to those who are willing to tell their stories of God. Homily discussion groups provide an opportunity for this conversation to take place. These are not homily preparation groups. Preachers still have the primary responsibility for studying the scriptures and writing the homily text. These discussion groups provide an opportunity for preachers and listeners to talk about how God's word speaks to their lived faith experience once they have a clearer understanding of what the scriptures proclaim. Preachers have the primary role of opening up the text for a fuller hearing. When the listeners can understand the context and purpose of the text, they can more easily offer reflections on how the word enters their lived experience.

How do people hear the beatitudes?

Consider, for example, how different individuals hear the preaching in Matthew 5:2-12, where Jesus proclaims "blessed" those who are poor in spirit, sorrowing, persecuted and insulted. This is a difficult text. Is Jesus saying we should seek out trials if we want to be considered blessed? Should we actually want to be insulted? Is it wrong to be happy? If a homily discussion group begins by trying to figure out what Jesus is talking about, it is likely to become bogged down in the process. Preachers can facilitate the group's task by sharing the results of their own study. Homily discussion groups typically operate on two levels. First, they spend time grappling with the meaning of the text. Second, they reflect on how this text touches their own spiritual journey.

The group begins by asking, "What is the purpose of this part of the Sermon on the Mount?" Preachers can help this phase of the discussion by explaining what is meant by "beatitude." Jesus is not urging disciples to begin seeking poverty and lowliness as ends in themselves, but he is rejoicing in those followers who are already experiencing the kingdom. Beatitudes are not commands to seek out lowliness. Instead they describe the state of followers who have already discovered the secret of discipleship: "In form, a beatitude is an exclamation of congratulations that recognizes an existing state of happiness...."[22] Jesus is describing the joy that followers have discovered in living the paradox of discipleship. When people are able to cease trying to fulfill their lives with money, power, success and all the other things that the world offers, when people find the Lord to be their real treasure, they are truly blessed. As the sermon continues, Jesus offers further teaching about true riches (Matthew 6:19ff.). The gospel tells us that as he concludes the sermon, he left the crowd spellbound at the power of his words.

Faith Questions

What does this message look like in people's lives? Have they really found a true treasure in Jesus, rather than in the many things the world says are necessary for happiness? For one young father of a newborn daughter, this word had special significance. He spoke of being at his wife's hospital bedside when the doctor told them that he wanted to prepare them before bringing in their new child. The little girl was born with a cleft palette. The father said both he and his wife felt their hearts sink. Like all parents, they wanted a perfect child. He said that when the little girl was brought in, he and his wife immediately saw her as a very beautiful gift from God. She was truly a treasure to them. Preachers who prepare homilies in isolation risk not hearing rich stories of how God's word enters the lives of listeners.

Conducting a Homily Preparation Group

Fulfilled in Your Hearing (36-38) outlines seven steps for a homily preparation group. The heart of the process is the listener's personal experience of the word. Preachers can consult the document for a complete description of the following steps.

A. Read the passages (15 minutes).

Starting with the gospel, one of the participants reads each reading slowly as others in the group jot down words, images, or phrases that catch their attention.

B. Share the words (10 minutes).

Participants read their list of words, images, and phrases. This part of the process is not a time of discussion. The preacher simply listens, especially noting any recurring patterns.

C. Exegete the text (10 minutes).

One group member presents a brief exegesis of the readings with emphasis on questions arising from historical criticism. (See Chapter Four for a brief treatment of historical criticism.)

D. Share the good news (10 minutes).

The next three steps are the heart of the process in that they deal with how the word is experienced in people's lives. Participants discuss what good news they think the first listeners heard in these readings. They then talk about their personal stories in light of these words of promise and hope.

E. Share the challenge these words offer (10 minutes).

At this point, participants are invited to talk about the community's brokenness. What are the obstacles to the good news? Where are the areas that need conversion?

F. Explore the consequences (5 minutes).

This section asks participants to think about how their lives would be different if the word were actually heard and heeded.

G. Give thanks and praise (5 minutes).

The process concludes in a spirit of prayer.

Preparation with Other Ministers

If you are using the appendix of this book, containing guidelines for working with a group of other preachers, you have already experienced the value of preparing homilies with peers in ministry. The group might wish to use the process outlined above. They may also choose to devote more of their preparation time to discussing insights from their study of the readings. The activity in the Discussion Session Guidelines for Chapter Two (p. 195) provides an exercise for examining the various moves in a passage of scripture. If your group is using this book in its suggested sequence, you already know that looking at a reading in terms of moves provides a fresh entrance into the text. If you have not yet dealt with Chapter Two, you may wish to try the activity section in the appendix as one element in preparing a future homily with peers.

4. Listening after Homilies

Feedback Forms

Printed feedback forms provide one method that preachers can use to hear from listeners who might be reluctant to engage in a face-to-face homily feedback session. A sample form appears at the end of this chapter (see pp. 136, Feedback from the Pews). Purchasing this book grants you the right to duplicate and distribute this form to your own congregation.

Paper-and-pencil evaluations have advantages and disadvantages. They are valuable in their ability to provide reactions from a relatively wide variety of respondents, since it would be possible for an entire parish to offer feedback on every homily, every Sunday. And if the forms are anonymous, some might feel free to offer comments to preachers that they would never say in person. Written responses also have disadvantages. Unless people fill out the form while they are still in the church, not all forms will be returned. Also, some people do not express themselves as clearly in writing as they do face-to-face, and forms do not allow preachers to interact with the listeners.

The sample form at the end of this chapter has a space for the name of the respondent. Knowing who filled out the form allows preachers to contact the persons who have provided particularly helpful comments. It may also help preachers choose potential members for a homily preparation or feedback group. Preachers may choose to offer listeners the option of remaining anonymous if individuals would otherwise not be inclined to respond openly and honestly.

Feedback Groups

Small groups involve more time and effort than paper-and-pencil surveys, but they also offer a level of qualitative feedback unavailable from printed forms. Respondents not only give their own reactions, but also have the opportunity to hear how the same homily has affected other listeners. The responses from one listener may trigger further reactions that would not have emerged if each listener responded in isolation. Three small group models are described here:

Faith-Questions Group

A small faith-questions group is designed to give preachers a sense of what other believers are hearing from God in a homily. This type of group does not evaluate the homily or the preacher. The process is concerned more with what was heard than with what was said. Preachers ask the listeners to respond to these, or similar, questions:

- Describe the God you heard in the homily.
- Did any aspect of the homily indicate how the preacher personally experienced God?
- Describe how your own faith experience is similar to the preacher's faith experience.
- Did the homily suggest anything about what God expects of you, the listener?

These questions often involve highly personal answers and comments. It is important to establish an atmosphere of trust in the group. The second question, for example, involves a personal judgment about the preacher's own faith. Whether preachers care to admit it or not, listeners are asking themselves, at least on some level of consciousness, whether their preachers believe what they are preaching. Recall the observation of Paul VI: "Modern man listens more willingly to witnesses than to teachers, and if he does listen to teachers, it is because they are also witnesses."[23]

In this type of process, participants need to know that the preachers and other group members will respect their reactions. Frequently, various group members will hear things in a homily that the preacher did not intend to communicate. Nor will group members always reach a consensus on what they have heard. Faith-questions groups show the richness involved when God's word is at work in listeners.

Listener Diaries

Roger Van Harn suggests another type of faith-centered feedback, which involves listeners keeping diaries. The reader may wish to consult a fuller description of this method in his book, *Pew Rights: For People Who Listen to Sermons*.[24] Briefly, the method involves asking a few parishioners to keep a daily diary for one week. Each day they make entries concerning the thoughts, feelings and experiences that they consider significant. Second, they enter any "words of faith and hope" they may have heard that day, which may or may not be from a religious source. On Sundays, they complete a series of questions based on the homily:

- The sermon was about…
- The sermon enabled me to believe that…
- The sermon asked that I…
- The sermon made me feel…[25]

Van Harn reports that the diaries offer a way for preachers to listen to the listeners both before and after the preaching event. The daily entries help preachers get a sense of what the listeners believe is important in their lives. The Sunday entries help preachers appreciate what the listeners actually heard in the homily. He offers several models for using this method, including a group session in which participants read and discuss their entries together.

Evaluation Groups

A third method for listening to listeners is the homily evaluation group. Unlike in the previous two models that focus on the faith response of the listeners, participants in an evaluation group are asked to give feedback on the preacher's performance. The same homily feedback form (Feedback from the Pews), designed to be distributed to parishioners, can provide questions and issues for discussion in an evaluation group. Preachers can ask a few persons who filled out this form to volunteer to meet and discuss their responses in a small group setting.

Peer Evaluation

The material in this section has dealt with feedback from listeners in the pews. Preachers using this book in a group setting have also experienced the value of peer feedback. Various discussion and workshop sections of the book have suggested specific questions to guide peer comments on homilies. The Homily Assessment form that follows is an instrument that group members can use to evaluate one another's homilies according to particular categories. Immediately following the assessment are directions for filling out the form and also descriptions of the various criteria. This instrument asks peers to evaluate a homily according to a set of specific preaching qualities and skills. It differs from the Feedback from the Pews form, which is intended for use in parish settings.

Copyright Notice

The following six pages may be photocopied or retyped and distributed by individuals who purchase this book. These forms may not be modified without the author's permission.

Homily Assessment		
	Rate (1-10)	Comments
Introduction		
So What?		
Organization and Central Idea		
Concrete		
Witness		
Scriptures		
Vocal Qualities		
Main Area for Improvement		
Miscellaneous Comments		
Overall Rating (1-10):		

from: Daniel E. Harris, C.M., *We Speak the Word of the Lord*

Homily Assessment Guidelines

Each item on the Homily Assessment form is rated on a scale of 1 to 10, 10 being the highest rating. The large spaces next to the rating area are for comments. Evaluators use this area to explain their rationale for the ratings.

Introduction   Does the introduction gain the interest of the congregation? Will listeners say, "This homily has something to offer me"?

So What?   Does the homily meet the realistic spiritual needs of the congregation? Does it make a difference? Has it left the people changed in some helpful way?

Organization and Central Idea   Is there one, simple, clear, central idea? Are the various movements or areas of development arranged in a way that makes the homily easy to follow?

Concrete   Does the preacher use enough examples and illustrations to help the congregation relate the message to life experience? Has the preacher avoided too much abstract language? Is the homily down to earth?

Witness   Is the preacher talking from personal faith experience? Witness can be explicit or implicit.

Scriptures   Is the homily rooted in one or more of the readings from the particular liturgy being celebrated? Is the preacher merely explaining the reading or proclaiming the message?

from: Daniel E. Harris, C.M., *We Speak the Word of the Lord*

Vocal Qualities   Is the voice animated and lively? Does the preacher sound enthusiastic about the message? Comments here might refer to rate, pitch, variety, volume, projection, etc.

Main Area for Improvement   What is one main area where the preacher can improve this homily? This comment can refer to a specific skill, element of content, organization, approach to scripture or any other issue that needs significant attention.

Miscellaneous Comments   The evaluator can add anything here that was not covered in earlier comments.

Overall Rating   This is the average of the ratings for each category.

from: Daniel E. Harris, C.M., *We Speak the Word of the Lord*

Feedback from the Pews

Preacher's Name_____   Your Name _____

Directions: This form is intended to provide preachers with a sense of how you listen to homilies. There are no right or wrong responses. Unless you have been directed otherwise, please respond only to the most recent homily you have heard (not to the preacher's homilies in general).

A. Circle the word that best expresses your reaction to the homily:

1. The message of this homily was very clear.
   Strongly   Agree   Uncertain   Disagree   Strongly
    Agree   Disagree

2. The preacher spoke on one main idea.
   Strongly   Agree   Uncertain   Disagree   Strongly
    Agree   Disagree

3. The homily was too long.
   Strongly   Agree   Uncertain   Disagree   Strongly
    Agree   Disagree

4. The homily was too short.
   Strongly   Agree   Uncertain   Disagree   Strongly
    Agree   Disagree

5. The homily helped me appreciate the scripture readings.
   Strongly   Agree   Uncertain   Disagree   Strongly
    Agree   Disagree

6. The preacher sounded interested in the message.
   Strongly   Agree   Uncertain   Disagree   Strongly
    Agree   Disagree

7. The homily kept my interest throughout.

Strongly   Agree   Uncertain   Disagree   Strongly
  Agree   Disagree

8. This homily will cause me to think more about its message.

Strongly   Agree   Uncertain   Disagree   Strongly
  Agree   Disagree

9. The preacher seemed to understand my concerns.

Strongly   Agree   Uncertain   Disagree   Strongly
  Agree   Disagree

10. The homily used interesting examples or stories.

Strongly   Agree   Uncertain   Disagree   Strongly
  Agree   Disagree

B. Complete the following sentences:

The main point of the homily was...

The part of the homily I most appreciated was...

I wish the preacher would have said more about...

The homily would have been better if...

C. Add any further comments you wish:

from: Daniel E. Harris, C.M., *We Speak the Word of the Lord*

Faith-Questions Homily Feedback Group

You are asked to help your preacher by discussing the following questions. After the homily tape has been played, respond to each question in terms of what you heard. There are no correct or incorrect answers. Your responses will help the preacher appreciate what listeners hear in terms of their own faith.

1. Describe the God you heard in the homily.

2. Did any aspect of the homily indicate how the preacher personally experiences God?

3. Describe how your own faith experience is similar to the preacher's faith experience.

4. Did the homily suggest anything about what God expects of you the listener?

from: Daniel E. Harris, C.M., *We Speak of the Word of the Lord*

Further Reading

Hilkert, Mary Catherine. *Naming Grace: Preaching and the Sacramental Imagination.* New York: Continuum, 1997.

Schlafer, David. J. *Surviving the Sermon: A Guide to Preaching for Those Who Have to Listen.* Boston: Cowley, 1992.

Troeger, Thomas. *The Parable of Ten Preachers.* Nashville: Abingdon, 1992. This creative narrative describes a group of homiletics students who wrestle with the demands of preaching a message that meets the needs of contemporary congregations. Their dialogue offers helpful insights on exegeting a congregation.

Van Harn, Roger E. *Pew Rights: For People Who Listen to Sermons.* Grand Rapids: Eerdmans, 1992.

Notes

1. David J. Schlafer, *Surviving the Sermon: A Guide to Preaching for Those Who Have to Listen* (Boston: Cowley, 1992), p. 4.

2. Schlafer, pp. 20-21.

3. Wallace E. Fisher, *Who Dares to Preach?: The Challenge of Biblical Preaching* (Minneapolis: Augsburg, 1979), p. 62.

4. Joan Deleplane, "The Living Word: An Overshadowing of the Spirit," in *In the Company of Preachers,* ed. Regina Siegfried and Edward Ruane (Collegeville, Minn.: Liturgical Press, 1993), pp. 148-49.

5. Louis Abelly, *The Life of the Venerable Servant of God Vincent de Paul,* vol. I, ed. John Rybolt (New Rochelle, N.Y.: New City, 1993), pp. 61-62.

6. Karl Rahner, *Theological Investigations,* vol. IV, trans. Kevin Smyth (Baltimore: Helicon Press, 1966), p. 260.

7. Kathleen Cannon, "Theology of the Word," in *The New Dictionary of Sacramental Worship,* ed. Peter E. Fink (Collegeville, Minn.: Liturgical Press, 1990), p. 1325.

8. Mary Catherine Hilkert, *Naming Grace: Preaching and the Sacramental Imagination* (New York: Continuum), 1997, pp. 48-49.

9. Stephen DeLeers, "Written Text Becomes Living Word: Official Roman Catholic Teaching on the Homily, 1963-93," in *Papers of the Annual Meeting of the Academy of Homiletics* (1996), p. 6.

10. Raymond Brown, "Preaching in the Acts of the Apostles," in *A New Look at Preaching*, ed. John Burke (Wilmington, Del.: Michael Glazier, 1983), pp. 64-65.

11. Roger E. Van Harn, *Pew Rights: For People Who Listen to Sermons* (Grand Rapids: Eerdmans, 1992), p. 31.

12. John Shea, *Stories of God [An Unauthorized Biography]* (Chicago: Thomas More, 1978), pp. 62-63.

13. Karl Rahner, "Priest and Poet," in *Theological Investigations*, vol. III, trans. Karl H. and Boniface Kruger (Baltimore: Helicon Press, 1967), p. 299.

14. Leonora Tubbs Tisdale, "Congregation," in *Concise Encyclopedia of Preaching*, ed. William H. Willimon and Richard Lischer (Louisville: Westminster/Knox, 1995), p. 87.

15. David G. Buttrick, "Who Is Listening?" in *Listening to the Word: Studies in Honor of Fred B. Craddock*, ed. Gail R. O'Day and Thomas G. Long (Nashville: Abingdon, 1993), pp. 189-206.

16. Buttrick, p. 193.

17. Hilkert, pp. 48-51.

18. Buttrick, p. 193.

19. Buttrick, p. 194.

20. Buttrick, p. 194.

21. Buttrick, p. 195.

22. Benedict T. Viviano, "The Gospel According to Matthew," in *The New Jerome Biblical Commentary*, ed. Raymond E. Brown, Joseph A. Fitzmyer, and Roland E. Murphy (Englewood Cliffs, N.J.: Prentice Hall, 1990), p. 640.

23. Paul VI, Address to the Members of the *Consilium de Laicis* (October 2, 1974) *Acta Apostolicae Sedis* 66 (1974): 568.

24. Van Harn, pp. 155-56.

25. Van Harn, p. 156.

Chapter Seven

Preaching the Prophetic Word

Offering a New Imagination

1. The Need for Prophetic Voices

A Wounded World

Shortly before his death, Joseph Cardinal Bernardin, Archbishop of Chicago, released *Called to Be Catholic: Church in a Time of Peril.* The National Pastoral Life Center prepared this document to foster dialogue among ever-widening factions within the Roman Catholic Church. The statement raised urgent issues facing the church, including: the role of women; the gap between church teaching on sexual morality and people's practice; the church's involvement in political issues, including its ministry to the poor, its concern for family life; and the church's ministry among African Americans, Latinos and Asians (*Called*, nn. 2-3).

Called to Be Catholic challenges believers to discuss their differences in a spirit of openness. Written guidelines alone will not produce the kind of personal conversion needed to deal with wounds in the church. The renewal of persons that is necessary for this openness grows within "the space created by praise and worship" (*Called*, n. 5).

Cardinal Bernardin's attempt to heal these wounds is a reminder that the church exists in a sinful world, and it is not exempt from the sins of injustice that permeate society. Many centuries have passed since the Acts of the Apostles described the spirit of mutual love and trust in the early Christian community. Although Acts presents an idealized picture of the church, it describes a people who at least strived to live as a community:

> They devoted themselves to the teaching of the apos-
> tles and to the communal life, to the breaking of bread
> and to the prayers.... All who believed were together and
> had all things in common; they would sell their proper-
> ty and possessions and divide them among all according
> to each one's need.
>
> Acts 2:42-44

Acts 4:32-37 describes how the first Christians sold their property and gave the proceeds to the poor. The next chapter recounts
how Ananias and Sapphira schemed to keep a portion of money for
themselves while they professed that they were giving everything
to the community (5:1-11).

The Church in a Sinful World

The church is part of the world that fosters unjust economic systems. A small percentage of the world's population enjoys great
wealth while the majority lives in poverty. Believers live in a world
of racism, sexism, physical and mental abuse, a growing hunger
among many for the vengeance of the death penalty for criminals,
and many other injustices. Walter Burghardt's *Preaching the Just
Word* offers a sobering analysis of these and other social wounds.[1]
Fulfilled in Your Hearing (n. 20) reminds preachers that their homilies interpret people's lives in light of the scriptures. Linking people's lives with God's word often involves pointing out the wounds
that characterize the lives of believers.

A Wounded Biblical World

A Story of Human Brokenness

Personal and communal sins of injustice did not originate in our
own time. The Book of Genesis describes the idyllic Eden, God's
wish for creation (2:8-25). It is not long before the first man and
woman choose their own will over their creator's plan (3:1-8). The
human story quickly degenerates into the story of the first murder
(4:8-17). Contemporaries who bemoan the sad state of our world
and invoke a return to "the old-time religion" have a selective reading of the Bible. Despite God's continual activity throughout salva-

tion history, God's people continue to lie, steal, murder and seek gods of their own making.

A Story of Personal Sin

King David, the former shepherd boy hand-picked by God to lead the people, is a prime example of the many wounded characters in salvation history (2 Samuel 5:1-6). He lusted after the beautiful Bathsheba and conceived a child with her (11:1-6). David attempted to arrange a conjugal visit between Bathsheba and her husband Uriah so that the sin could be kept secret. When that plan failed, David arranged to have Uriah killed in battle (11:6-14). This story of lust and treachery sounds like today's television soap operas or afternoon talk shows. God sends Nathan the prophet to bring the secret sin into the open. Nathan tells David the story of a wicked rich man who, in order to feed guests, steals a ewe from a poor man. After David agrees that the rich man has acted despicably, the prophet proclaims, "You are the man!" (2 Samuel 12:7).

Stories of Injustice

In the days of Amos, Israel had become a perverse nation, not just in terms of personal sin but as a people who practiced large-scale injustice. The prophet chastises the women of Samaria who are oppressive toward the poor (Amos 4:1). Amos condemns the corrupt rulers of Judah and Israel. While the poor continue to suffer, the wealthy are "[l]ying upon beds of ivory, stretched comfortably on their couches..." (6:4).

Centuries after these ancient prophets, we continue to hear similar concerns in the scriptures. Paul warned the people of Corinth that they made a mockery of the Lord's Supper by ignoring the poor in their midst. Paul reprimands the wealthier members who gathered to share fine food and drink while others went hungry (1 Corinthians 11:17-22). The scriptures tell many more stories of injustice. They also relate stories of persons God has sent to call the people back to faithfulness.

2. Prophetic Voices

Prophetic Voices in Scripture

There is a common misconception about the term "prophet."

Biblical prophets were not self-righteous, angry persons who lashed out against injustice from personal disgust. This characterization fails to captures the spirit and mission of biblical prophets. Authentic prophets never spoke on their own authority. Prophets spoke for another. They revealed the mind and will of God.[2]

The Scandal of Biblical Justice

Biblical prophets proclaimed *justice*. What did the prophets mean by "justice"? It is not what contemporary Americans mean by legal justice. Nor is biblical justice what moral theologians call "distributive justice," that is, giving to each person what is his or her right. God's word calls people beyond what is merely fair or deserved. Walter Burghardt calls this the "scandal" of the scriptures. The Bible challenges believers to treat one another and all of creation as God has treated them. Biblical justice is not about rules but about relationships.[3]

The Logic of Superabundance

According to Paul Ricoeur, the prophets, including Jesus, did not preach limited moral directives. They spoke with a "logic of superabundance" that broke open the imagination to new possibilities. In Romans, Paul repeats the logic of superabundance with his formula, "how much more" (Romans 5:9,10,15,17).[4] He declares, for example, that if death entered the world through one person's sin, it is all the more certain that eternal life enters the world through Christ (Romans 5:17).

Jesus shows the logic of superabundance by teaching his disciples that love is not a matter of treating others only as they deserve. True disciples love others as generously as God loves:

> "You have heard that it was said, 'You shall love your neighbor and hate your enemy.' But I say to you, love your enemies, and pray for those who persecute you, that you may be children of your heavenly Father, for he makes his sun rise on the bad and the good, and causes rain to fall on the just and the unjust."
>
> Matthew 5:43-46

Some potential followers were not ready to love others and creation as God loves. When a rich man came up to the Teacher asking what he must do to be saved, Jesus invited him to imagine a life that goes beyond the commandments. What if he would sell all his many possessions and then follow Jesus? The man walked away, unable to imagine this new possibility. Jesus takes the occasion to say how hard it is for the rich to accept the kingdom of God. It is impossible to enter the kingdom unless one relies on God. The last verse of the account describes what is necessary if one is to accept the logic of superabundance. "All things are possible for God" (Mark 10:17-28).

Prophetic Voices in the Church

Vatican Council II: In addition to the prophetic voices in the scriptures, God continues to call people to live justly through the church's living tradition. Vatican II, in the *Pastoral Constitution on the Church in the Modern World* (n. 9), echoes the voices of the ancient prophets:

> The hungry nations cry out to their affluent neighbors; women claim parity with men in fact as well as of rights, where they have not already obtained it; farmers and workers insist not just on the necessities of life but also on the opportunity to develop by their labor their personal talents and to play their due role in organizing economic, social political, and cultural life.

Justice in the World

Some Christians believe that the church has no legitimate role in political issues. As they put it, "The church should stay out of politics and stick to preaching the gospel. We come to church to hear about God and how to live as good Catholics. We do not come to church to hear about politics." The 1971 Synod of Bishops challenges preachers and listeners to reflect on the centrality of justice in an authentic proclamation of the gospel. Preaching, the bishops remind the church, is not simply a matter of an individual's relationship with God. Justice is a constitutive dimension of preaching:

Action on behalf of justice and participation in the transformation of the world fully appear to us as a constitutive dimension of the preaching of the Gospel, or, in other words, of the Church's mission for the redemption of the human race and its liberation from every oppressive situation.[5]

3. New Imaginations

Postmodern Imagination

The prophetic word faces a special challenge for contemporary preachers and listeners. Walter Brueggemann reminds preachers and listeners that they hear and proclaim the scriptures from a *postmodern* viewpoint. The *modern* era, shaped in the seventeenth and eighteenth centuries, was a world comfortable with scientific and empiricist objectivity. Contemporary people, believers and nonbelievers alike, have grown skeptical toward the dogmatic, objective, domineering worldview of the modern era. A recent trend in communication strategies in both the Democratic and Republican parties illustrates the shift in thinking. It is now common practice for both parties to include the personal stories of particular men, women or children who are struggling to live the American dream. Political conventions use video clips to show these personal stories. Sometimes these average Americans themselves stand on stage with their candidates to describe their experiences in their own words.

In the postmodern atmosphere, preachers can no longer afford to take refuge in abstract, dogmatic pronouncements. In this era the preacher offers images and metaphors that allow people to imagine a new vision of the self, the community and the world. This new imagination is expressed not in the sweeping universal rhetoric of the past, but in the local, oral, particular and timely.[6]

Funding a New Imagination

In his *Texts Under Negotiation: The Bible and Postmodern Imagination*, Brueggemann argues that preachers fund a new imagination, "to provide the pieces, material, and resources out of which a new world can be imagined."[7] Authentic prophetic preaching offers an alternate imagination filled with hope. This new imagination involves an alternate self, community and world:

- *imagine* a self defined not by consumerism, an absolute individualism with no responsibility to the community, nor by what the individual can produce. The new self finds worth in a loving God.
- *imagine* a world not of power struggles, but one that reflects the covenant between God and people symbolized by the rainbow of Genesis.
- *imagine* a community not of hopelessness, but one that believes God is with God's people.[8]

Dismantling a Static Religion

Part of the process of offering a new imagination involves the uncomfortable task of dismantling those dimensions of a religiosity that no longer allow God to be God. Prophetic voices announce that the dominant culture has reduced religion to "static triumphalism" and imposed a "politics of oppression and exploitation."[9] Brueggemann describes a static religion as one that controls the gods who in turn justify the politics that serve the kings. A prophet announces a "religion of God's freedom with the politics of human justice."[10] In a static religion, God serves the views and aims of the state's power brokers. A free God can hear the cries of the poor.

Jesus is the ultimate dismantler of the old static religion and the politics of oppression. In the spirit of a postmodern appeal to specific instances rather than generalizations, Brueggemann cites gospel images of Jesus that allow the reader to form a new imagination:

- The birth of Jesus dismantles the old trappings of kingly privilege. Matthew's infancy narrative clearly shows Jesus' solidarity with the poor.
- Herod (the old king) is seen as powerless in contrast to Jesus, the true king (Matthew 2:11).
- The ministry of Jesus dismantles the old order: Jesus forgives sins, evoking amazement from the crowds (Mark 2:1-12). The old order did not make room for such generous forgiveness of sin, since the social structures controlled the machinery of forgiveness.

Healing on the Sabbath revoked the Sabbath's power to enslave people (Mark 3:1-6). Jesus eats with outcasts (Mark 2:15-17). This was unheard of in the old order. Jesus displayed a shocking attitude toward the Temple, especially in foretelling its destruction. In criticizing the Temple, Jesus attacked the doctrine of Jewish election (Mark 11:15-19; John 2:18-22).

- The crucifixion is the ultimate criticism of the royal consciousness. Jesus freely embraces the very death that the old order has become too numb to face.[11]

The Word of God Calls for a Change of Mind

The Letter to the Hebrews calls God's word "living and effective, sharper than any two-edged sword, penetrating even between soul and spirit, joints and marrow, and able to discern reflections and thoughts of the heart" (Hebrews 4:12). What if the two-edged sword becomes dulled and ineffective because complacent listeners refuse to hear? What if preachers or listeners want God to fit into neat categories that neither challenge nor disturb comfortable religious lives?

Preachers and congregations settle into apathy when religion becomes a matter of simply knowing the right answers. For these comfortable Christians, the scriptures no longer call for any real change nor conversion. The gospel becomes a safe, consoling message. If the complacent do hear a call to conversion, it is "those other sinners" who need to change. Raymond Brown warns that such complacency removes the important "offense" of scripture in which God calls for true *metanoein*, that is, "to change one's mind."[12]

The Word of God Disorients the Comfortable

The parables, hyperbole and extreme sayings of Jesus disorient hearers. These challenging words then reorient listeners to a new imagination, a new way of seeing things.[13] The parable of the workers in the vineyard (Matthew 20:1-17) is especially disorienting for American ears. We rightly value an honest day's pay for an honest day's work. Critics of Affirmative Action argue that the program gives minorities something they have not *earned*. This parable of Jesus describes how workers received the same pay whether they labored all day or only one hour. The last verse of the parable surprises all who judge the story as unfair: "Are you envious because I am generous?" This parable, and much of what Jesus said and did, challenges listeners to accept a generous God who does not act in the calculating ways that people usually treat one another.

4. Prophecy versus Moralism

The Tendency to Moralize

When preachers address the wounded church, with its individual and communal sins of injustice, they often resort to mere moralism. Moral guidelines play an important role in the formation of believers. Conscientious disciples want to live a moral life in accord with the practices of the religious community. Parents and teachers, for example, often find themselves in the role of moral guides as they help children develop a healthy sense of responsibility. Moralism, though, falls far short of authentic gospel preaching. It merely points out the sin and offers specific remedies.

Moralism, Grace and Jesus

It is not enough for preachers simply to tell people how God expects them to behave. Moralizing assumes that people can live virtuous lives once they understand God's expectations. It excludes the role of grace. God's word does not rely on human will power to produce its effect in people's hearts. Nor does it simply tell people that they *should* be disciples. God's word, which is grace-filled, offers people the *power* to be authentic disciples. God's word contains grace.[14]

Jesus instructed men and women about the moral consequences of discipleship. He told former sinners to sin no more. Was Jesus being a mere moralist in these instances? According to moral theologian Charles Bouchard, "Jesus repeatedly makes it clear that he has come to save people, to make them new, to convert them. He is not interested only in changing actions, goals, norms, or rules."[15] When Nicodemus came to Jesus at night, he learned what it meant to live in the light. Jesus proclaimed that anyone who wishes to be part of the reign of God must be "born from above" (John 3:3). When Nicodemus protests that someone cannot reenter the womb and be born again, Jesus replies: "...I say to you, no one can enter the kingdom of God without being born of water and Spirit" (John 3:5). Jesus has come to do much more than offer a new set of rules. He has come to give new life to persons. The following examples illustrate the distinction between simply moralizing on behavior, and preaching Jesus Christ who is the power to follow the law.

Example of Moralizing

On this Sunday we celebrate the feast of the Presentation of Our Lord. As that small child is brought into the Temple, I cannot help but think of the many tiny lives that never see the light of day. Every day in our country unborn children are killed in abortion clinics. A woman, with or without the cooperation of the father, has decided, "It is my body and I can do what I want with it." The *Catechism of the Catholic Church* leaves no doubt about the issue. "Human life must be respected and protected absolutely from the moment of conception" (n. 2270). Later the catechism reminds Catholics that anyone who formally cooperates in an abortion incurs excommunication (n. 2272).

Recently a parishioner complained to me that the church does not make that excommunication clear enough. People need to know that abortion is a most serious sin. I want to make it abundantly clear now. One who procures an abortion or who formally cooperates in that sin is excommunicated!... [The homily continues explaining why abortion is such a serious sin.]

Example of Prophetic Preaching

Mary and Joseph, like all good Jewish parents, bring their firstborn son to the Temple for the ceremony of purification. Simeon and Anna have seen this ritual countless times. Today their aging eyes light up with excitement. This child is someone different. This child is the one they have been waiting to see. This child is the one who will be the salvation of all people.

Although the purification ritual happened long ago, Jesus, the light of the nations, is very much with us now. Jesus, purified in the Temple long ago, enters our lives through baptism. Our baptism transforms us into a new people. We have a dignity as sons and daughters of God. Our dignity does not come from the color of our skin or the size of our bank balance. Jesus has made each of us precious—period. No exceptions. We even have dignity before we are born.... [The homily continues describing respect for life as a consequence of one's relationship with Christ.]

The Power to Follow the Law

Some preachers may find the example of moralism more attractive than the example of prophetic preaching. They may prefer the way that moralism uncompromisingly names the sin of abortion. The example points to a serious problem and supports the condemnation by appealing to legitimate authority. Moralism is not authentic preaching. Even when it expresses the truth with great clarity and passion, moralism cannot produce true conversion in the listener. Moralistic appeals simply tell people what is wrong in their lives and what they should do about the sin. Authentic prophetic preaching, on the other hand, goes beyond merely naming the sin. It proclaims Christ who is the forgiveness of sin. Authentic preaching brings with it the grace to live moral lives.

The brief homily segments above might give the impression that moralism is specific and concrete, but prophetic preaching simply talks about Jesus in general terms. This conclusion misses the essential difference between the two approaches. Prophetic preaching is also specific and concrete in identifying the consequences of discipleship. It can deal with issues such as abortion, poverty, racism and sexism in very specific language. These issues are real life consequences of discipleship. Moralists merely describe the concrete consequences without preaching Christ who is the power to live them. This was an important distinction for Martin Luther's understanding of preaching.

5. Law and Gospel

Luther's Insight

Martin Luther insisted that authentic preaching is impossible if sermons simply tell congregations what they need to know or do to be saved. For Luther, authentic preaching encompasses both law and gospel. Preaching, which goes beyond instruction in law, proclaims the saving power of Christ who has made us into a new people able to follow God's law. Without the power of Christ, the law can only judge and condemn. Chapter One introduced Luther's *postils*, resources written to guide preachers in studying the scriptures and proclaiming them with the power of the saving Christ. This section briefly describes Luther's notion of law and gospel. He considered this issue to be so important that he believed that any preacher who could properly distinguish law and gospel deserved to be considered "a doctor of Holy Writ."[16]

Law and Gospel in the Scriptures

Luther observed many contradictions in the way the scriptures describe salvation. In some passages, salvation seems entirely up to people's efforts. In other places, salvation seems entirely up to God. Preachers can resolve these contradictions when they realize that the scriptures comprise both law and gospel, "two entirely different doctrines."[17] In Exodus 20:1-18, God gives the people the Ten Commandments. The next three chapters further specify these commandments as they apply to treatment of slaves, injury to persons and property, the proper keeping of religious feasts and many other aspects of daily life. Standing on their own, passages like these seem to suggest that people's salvation depends upon simply following the commandments. In other places, God's word clearly proclaims that salvation is God's work, not the work of people. Human effort is vain and useless because it the Lord who saves:

> Unless the Lord build the house,
> they labor in vain who build....
> It is vain for you to rise early,
> and put off your rest at night,
> To eat bread earned by hard toil—
> All this God gives to his beloved in sleep.
>
> Psalm 127:1-2

Luther believed that the Letter to the Romans was the key to understanding the relationship between the law that judges and the gospel that saves:

> Now the righteousness of God has been manifested
> apart from the law, though testified to by the law and the
> prophets, the righteousness of God through faith in Jesus
> Christ for all who believe. For there is no distinction; all
> have sinned and are deprived of the glory of God. They
> are justified freely by his grace through the redemption
> in Christ Jesus (Rom.3:21-25).

Disciples of Luther continue to hold that *both law and gospel have
a positive function* in preaching. The Lutheran *Formula of Concord*
affirms: "The law is a divine doctrine which teaches what is right
and God-pleasing and which condemns everything that is sinful
and contrary to God's will."[18] The gospel is "the doctrine that teaches what a man who has not kept the law and is condemned by it
should believe, namely, that Christ has satisfied and paid for all
guilt and without man's merit has obtained and won for him forgiveness of sins...."[19]

Gospel Precedence in Preaching

Preaching the law points out a hearer's need for the saving power
of the gospel. Despite this value for one's faith journey, the law
never takes precedence over the gospel in authentic preaching.
Preachers who give prominence to the law, or who attempt to balance both law and gospel, "pervert" the word.[20] A Lutheran
homiletics professor commented that he uses a red highlighter to
indicate the law in the manuscripts of students' sermons, and a yellow highlighter to indicate the gospel. Too often the red predomi-
nates, with only a hint of yellow. Recall the youth minister mentioned in Chapter Two who observed that preachers are often specific when telling young people what to avoid as Catholics: Young
Catholics must not use illegal drugs, participate in gangs nor engage
in sexual activity before marriage. Do preachers tell them what they
can do once they believe in Jesus Christ? Do they preach a Christ
who is also good news?

Preaching Christ

Law and gospel preaching is an integral part of the Lutheran tradition. This stance toward the scriptures and preaching can provide

a fresh approach for Roman Catholics and preachers in other Christian traditions. All ministers of the word can benefit from Martin Luther's insight that authentic preaching proclaims the saving power of Christ. Preaching is never content only to tell people what Christ would have them know and believe.

6. Guidelines for Preaching the Prophetic Word

A. Preach God and Nothing Less

Walter Burghardt's Preaching the Just Word program is a retreat-workshop aimed at helping preachers more effectively proclaim biblical justice. Burghardt noted that people do not come to the Eucharist for ethical lectures. People yearn to hear a word from God that speaks to their present life situation.[21] Preachers who intend to minister with credibility in contemporary society need to know ethics. There are times and places for lectures, but worship is the time for allowing God to speak to God's people.

B. Preach for Change

Biblical prophets preached conversion. Contemporary social justice preaching not only names the sin in the community, it offers the power to imagine a new just world. Burghardt calls preachers to proclaim the just word in a way that calls for action. Effective social justice preaching moves listeners to identify the justice issues in their midst, discover what resources they have to address these issues and develop concrete plans of action.[22]

C. Preach As One Who Lives Justice

Paul the preacher realized that if he spoke with great eloquence but did not have love, his preaching was worthless (1 Corinthians 13:1). The power of prophetic preaching lies not in fiery rhetoric, but in the presence of God who speaks in the preached word. Preachers who are effective in proclaiming justice are themselves hearers of the just word. Those who live biblical justice are those who strive to love others as God has loved creation and all creatures.

D. Preach with Compassion

The sample homily segment in this chapter that dealt with abortion quoted the catechism's strong condemnation of those who take the lives of the unborn. The same paragraph in the catechism adds that this penalty stresses the gravity of the sin for individuals and society. The implication is that the church does not condemn the sinner. "The Church does not thereby intend to restrict the scope of mercy" (n. 2272). Preachers sometimes fail to include mercy and compassion when they preach a prophetic message. God's word does not leave people steeped in sin. Authentic prophetic preaching always offers hope.

E. Preach to the Whole Church

The church has a predilection for the poor. The Bible describes God's special love for the *anawim* whom the world shuns and oppresses. The desire to identify with the oppressed has led some to choose life among the poor that they may "share their bitter cares" (*Apostolic Exhortation on the Renewal of Religious Life*, n. 18). Those who identify with the poor face the challenge of preaching to the entire church. They preach to the oppressors and the oppressed. It is not only the *anawim* who need to hear the good news. All people are marginalized in some sense.[23]

F. Preach Hope

Describing the many gifts of the Spirit, Paul names prophecy to be especially important for building up the church. The prophet speaks to encourage and to console (1 Corinthians 14:3). Gospel ministers who share Paul's compulsion to preach do not condemn their congregations with a sense of sin and injustice. Biblical prophets ultimately offered a message of hope. At the beginning of his prophetic ministry the prophet Isaiah proclaims:

> Come now, let us set things right,
> says the Lord:
> Though your sins be like scarlet,
> they may become white as snow;
> Though they be crimson red,
> they may become white as wool.
>
> Isaiah 1:18

G. Sample Homily: God's Presence in All People

The following homily is from a liturgy celebrated at a wealthy
suburban parish north of Los Angeles. It illustrates how one can
introduce social justice consequences without the heavy handed-
ness that too readily turns off a congregation. The homily concludes not on a note of condemnation but on a note of hope.

In the first reading (Malachi 3:1-4), the Lord promises to send a
messenger to prepare the way. In the second (Hebrews 2:14-18),
Jesus did not come into the world to help angels. He came as a man
of flesh and blood to save people. The short form of the gospel for
this feast, the Presentation (Luke 2:1,22-34), begins with the parents
of Jesus bringing him to the Temple for the purification ceremony.
Simeon, speaking under the influence of the Holy Spirit, blesses
God for revealing this "light for revelation to the Gentiles, and
glory for your people Israel."

[Longings] A few years ago, Hollywood re-released the
film *Star Wars*. The news reported phenomenal interest
in the film as people lined up all over the country to see
it. On a television interview, the program's host asked a
film historian, "Why was this film so popular when it
first came out, and why is there such an interest in it
now?" The historian responded that he believes *Star
Wars* taps a deep longing for religious hope. It was first
released shortly after the Watergate scandal, a time when
many people were feeling cynical and disillusioned. Suddenly this movie comes on the scene. It was a story about
good people fighting against an evil oppressor. The hero-
ic characters had "the force" on their side. A great power
protected those on the side of goodness and justice.

People need faith when they feel oppressed. They
have a longing for some power that can deliver them
from trials. This is a powerful longing. During the lam-
entable time of slavery in our country's history, one
could hear the longing for deliverance in the slaves'
songs. One of these songs, for example, pleads, "Swing
low, sweet chariot, comin' for to carry me home." The

deep religious faith of the slaves was a faith of longing.

[People Long for Deliverance] We hear that same longing in our first reading today from the prophet Malachi. God's chosen people knew slavery, too. They had known prejudice and persecution through centuries. At times in their history they were slaves in Egypt. At last they came to experience freedom and a new homeland through the Exodus. Only a short time later they were once again captives. This time they were slaves in Babylon. In the era of this ancient prophecy from Malachi, even some of the religious leaders had become corrupt. The people longed for deliverance. It is good news indeed when they hear that the Lord will again visit this people. The Lord will enter the Jerusalem Temple and purify the people. It is a ringing promise. Malachi and the ancient people of this prophecy could never have imagined what that deliverance would finally look like.

[The Presentation in the Temple] We who have heard this gospel see where God's promises lead. We heard how the Lord entered the Temple to answer ancient longings. On this feast of the Presentation, the parents of Jesus bring their firstborn child to the Jerusalem Temple, according to religious custom. There in the Temple, a wise old man named Simeon immediately recognizes the fulfillment of the promise. He utters a prayer saying now he can die—he has seen the promise fulfilled. Not only is this child the deliverance of Israel, he is a light to all the nations. This child fulfills the promise first given to the chosen people. This child is a light to all people, Jew and Gentile alike. We celebrated Jesus as the light of the nations with the candles we blessed at the start of this Eucharist.

[Jesus Embraced All of Creation] The Letter to the Hebrews, our second reading, proclaims that in this child, God has truly become one of us. Jesus has embraced our humanness. God embraces our world. Our God is not an aloof God who sits up in heaven dropping occasional blessings upon us. Despite what *Star Wars* would have us believe, our God is not a vague force, an elusive power that guides us. God is with us. Jesus eats and drinks, gets tired, gets angry at times, laughs, and is tempted to sin as we are. He has embraced us and our world. This is the good news of the Presentation.

[Injustice] Unfortunately, our world has not fully embraced Jesus. Since I have moved to California, I have seen stories of at least one act of brutal violence in the Los Angeles news every day. On many days, there are stories of one or more murders. You and I don't have to watch the news to know that many people end the lives of the unborn each day. A moral theologian friend of mine said years ago that once abortion became legal, euthanasia, so-called mercy killing, would be the next legal debate, and that has happened. Our news broadcasts report stories about the homeless, battered women, racial bigotry and hatred. Jesus has embraced this world of ours, but our world has not fully embraced Jesus. Jesus is the light in our darkness, but too many continue to live in the darkness.

[Runaway Children] We have seen the sad images in the news that show emaciated African children who are innocent victims of tribal violence. While those pictures move us, they probably no longer surprise us. I was surprised, however, by a book I received in the mail from Covenant House, the organization that cares for runaway children. The stories in this book sound as if they came from Third World countries, from places where entire peoples have always known poverty. The stories concern our own children, perhaps children who grew up in this neighborhood. Despite how our country publicly calls children our greatest treasure, obviously the world has not yet embraced Jesus. Sister Mary Rose McGeady, who runs the Covenant House shelters for runaway children, dedicated the book "to the 1,000,000 homeless children who slept on the streets last year, scared, cold, hungry, alone and most of all, desperate to find someone who cares."[24] Think of the children who grow up around gang violence. Little children commonly plan their own funerals because they know it probably will not be long until they are victims. Jesus has embraced the world, but not all the world has embraced Jesus.

[What Can We Do?] We live in a very broken world. Perhaps some here are thinking, "What can we do about all this?" That is a fair question. If a single homily could answer that question we would have had a perfect world long ago. There are plenty of good people in this community who would gladly fix it all if they knew how. There are no easy answers for the complex issues of poverty and injustice. If this feast of the Presentation means anything, it means that we cannot celebrate a Jesus who embraces our human world only within our church buildings. Jesus also embraces the homeless, the poor, and the abused who perhaps do not feel welcome inside our churches.

[One Small Step] What can we do? We can begin by trying to see our world with the fresh vision that comes from believing in Jesus. We can ask for a genuine change of heart. Our inner conversion may begin with just one small step. The well-known motto of the Christophers provides a clue: "It is better to light one small candle than to curse the darkness." We did light candles as we began this liturgy of the Presentation. We are celebrating Jesus as a light to the nations. Perhaps it is enough simply to hear Jesus invite us today to carry the light outside this church. Perhaps it is enough to tell the Lord we truly want to be people who can see his face in the faces of those who are in need. That is a small step. A few steps can be the start of a very important journey.

[Eucharist] Jesus, presented in the Temple two thousand years ago, is the Christ of this Eucharist. The Jesus who embraced our world back then, continues to embrace ordinary bread and wine today. As we receive the Lord here, let us ask him to show each of us how we can be people who spread his light to others.

Further Reading

Burghardt, Walter J. *Preaching the Just Word*. New Haven: Yale University Press, 1996.

Synod of Bishops. "Justice in the World." November 30, 1971. *Official Catholic Teachings: Social Justice*. Ed., Vincent P. Mainelli. Wilmington, Del.: McGrath, 1978, 284-302. [This document is also found in other official publications.]

Notes

1. Walter J. Burghardt, *Preaching the Just Word* (New Haven: Yale University Press, 1996).

2. Bruce Vawter, "Introduction to Prophetic Literature," in *The New Jerome Biblical Commentary*, ed. Raymond Brown, Joseph Fitzmyer, and Roland Murphy (Englewood Cliffs, N.J.: Prentice Hall, 1990, 1968), p. 197.

3. Burghardt, pp. 2-3.

4. Paul Ricoeur, *Figuring the Sacred*, trans. David Pellauer; ed. Mark I. Wallace (Minneapolis: Fortress Press, 1995), p. 279.

5. Synod of Bishops, "Justice in the World," (November 30, 1971) in *Official Catholic Teachings: Social Justice*, ed. Vincent P. Mainelli (Wilmington, Del.: McGrath, 1978), p. 285.

6. Walter Brueggemann, *Texts Under Negotiation: The Bible and Postmodern Imagination* (Minneapolis: Fortress Press, 1993), pp. 8-9.

7. Brueggemann, p. 20.

8. Brueggemann, pp. 49-53.8.

9. Brueggemann, p. 16.

10. Brueggemann, p. 17.

11. Brueggemann, pp. 81-85.

12. Raymond Brown, "Preaching in the Acts of the Apostles," in *A New Look at Preaching*, ed. John Burke (Wilmington, Del.: Michael Glazier, 1983), p. 67.

13. Ricoeur, pp. 281-83.

14. Karl Rahner, "The Word and the Eucharist," in *Theological Investigations*, vol. IV, trans. Kevin Smyth (Baltimore: Helicon Press, 1966), pp. 259-60.

15. Charles Bouchard, "Authentic Preaching on Moral Issues," in

In the Company of Preachers, ed. Regina Siegfried and Edward Ruane (Collegeville, Minn.: Liturgical Press, 1993), p. 196.

16. C. Walther, *God's No and God's Yes: The Proper Distinction Between Law and Gospel*, cond., Walter C. Pieper (St. Louis: Concordia, 1973), p. 13.

17. Walther, p. 13.

18. Theodore G. Tappert, ed., "The Formula of Concord," in *The Book of Concord: The Confessions of the Evangelical Lutheran Church* (Philadelphia: Muhlenberg, 1959), p. 478.

19. Tappert, p. 478.

20. Walther, p. 117.

21. George Anderson, "Preaching the Just Word: An Interview With Walter J. Burghardt," *America* 175.9 (1996): 11.

22. Burghardt, p. 59.

23. James Empereur and Christopher Kiesling, *The Liturgy That Does Justice*, Theology and Life Series 33 (Collegeville, Minn.: Liturgical Press, 1990), p. 95.

24. Mary Rose McGeady, *Are You Out There God?* (USA: Covenant House, 1996).

Chapter Eight

Daily Homilies, Funerals, Weddings

Preaching on Weekdays and Special Occasions

1. Preaching at Weekday Liturgies

Most of this book deals with preaching at Sunday liturgies. On Sundays the local church gathers as the people of God to celebrate the Eucharist. Conscientious preachers devote a great deal of time and energy in preparing for this weekly liturgy. Smaller groups of Catholics participate in daily Eucharist, but few ministers have the time to prepare daily homilies as thoroughly as they do the Sunday preaching. This final chapter offers guidelines for preaching on a daily basis. It also concerns preaching at weddings, funerals, and children's liturgies.

Liturgical Guidelines for Daily Homilies

Homilies at weekday liturgies are a relatively new part of the church's worship; they emerged at the time of the Second Vatican Council. The *Constitution on the Sacred Liturgy* called homilies integral to the liturgy. To stress their importance, the document specified that preachers may not omit homilies on Sundays and holy days without a serious reason (n. 52). Homilies during weekday liturgies were considered to be optional, but recommended (*Code of Canon Law*, n.767 S3). In practice, most weekday liturgies feature a brief homily.

Keeping Daily Homilies Authentic

Although daily homilies are brief, they are still an integral part of the liturgy. Daily homilies, like those on Sunday, find their source in the scriptures or other liturgical texts and lead the congregation into a fuller participation at the Eucharist. Weekday homilies are not brief commentaries on the saint who is celebrated at a particular Eucharist. The guidelines for Sunday homilies discussed in this book also apply to weekday preaching. On the other hand, daily homilies present unique challenges and opportunities.

Exegeting the Weekday Congregation

Chapter Six, Listening to the Listeners, presented guidelines for exegeting the congregation. The weekday Eucharist offers other opportunities and challenges to link the lives of the congregation with the scriptures. Recall that *Fulfilled in Your Hearing* (20) states that the preacher "does not so much attempt to explain the scriptures as to interpret the human situation through the Scriptures." Weekday congregations differ from Sunday assemblies in several ways:

- A small segment of the church attends daily Eucharist.
- Some people attend on their way to work.
- Others are retirees.
- Usually the same people attend every day.
- Weekday congregations participate by choice, not from obligation.
- They are more familiar with the scriptures and the liturgy than many who participate on Sunday.
- Many in the congregation know one another and know the preacher.

Preparing with the Congregation

Because preachers usually know those who attend weekday Eucharist, they have a greater opportunity to include the voices of the listeners in their homilies. Chapter Six offers several models for seeking feedback and preparing homilies with the congregation. Since people who attend daily Eucharist often know one another and know the preacher, they would likely be at ease meeting in these groups. The insights from these discussions would also be helpful for preachers in preparing Sunday homilies.

Creative Preaching

Daily Eucharist offers opportunities for creative approaches that would be more difficult at the Sunday Eucharist. Preachers at daily Eucharist, for example, can involve the congregation by asking questions. A member of the congregation who has a special devotion to the saint honored at a feast or memorial might present a brief talk before the Eucharist. Liturgical guidelines say that the presider is the usual preacher of the homily and the faithful should not add comments. While respecting these guidelines, preachers have a great deal of room for creatively celebrating the word at weekday liturgies.

Preparing Daily Homilies

How can busy ministers consistently prepare themselves for preaching every day? One approach to preparing daily homilies involves two phases. In the *remote* phase, the preacher spends time throughout the day reflecting on the readings for the next day's liturgy. In the brief *proximate* phase, which involves about thirty minutes, the homily takes shape in outline form.

Remote Preparation

1. Read both readings early in the day. Listening to the readings early in the day allows the word to germinate in the preacher. Some preachers read the texts into a tape recorder and listen to the tapes while driving between appointments.

2. Spend time in prayer with the readings. Lectionary readings provide a rich source for a preacher's daily meditation. When preachers have prayed the word, not just studied the texts, their homilies become the word of witnesses who share what they have heard and believe.

3. Choose a general theme. After prayer, choose a general theme or direction for the homily. This narrowing process usually means preachers will limit themselves to one reading, often one movement within the reading.

Proximate Preparation

1. Brainstorm on the theme. Recall that brainstorming involves writing down the thoughts, images, quotations, and experiences

that come to mind concerning the general theme.

2. Choose a central idea. Daily homilies, like all homilies, have only one central idea, which can be expressed in a simple sentence.

3. Reflect on personal experience. Where have I, the preacher, experienced the central idea? Experiences readily come to mind if the preacher has prayed over the readings earlier in the day.

4. Consider the congregation's experience. Ask where the congregation experiences the central idea. Since preachers usually know the people who attend daily Eucharist, this exegesis of the congregation is often easier than when preparing a Sunday homily.

5. Outline the homily. The chapter on creating homilies urges preachers to write a full homily text in an oral style. Full manuscripts are seldom feasible for daily preaching. A brief outline will serve to guide a preacher in proclaiming the fruits of the remote and proximate phases.

Keeping Daily Homilies Fresh and Brief

Refer to Chapters Two and Three for suggestions on keeping homilies lively and fresh. In particular, recall Edward Fischer's observation that even wonderful news becomes stagnant and tedious unless it is presented with distinction.[1]

Daily homilies are brief compared to Sunday preaching. Edward Fischer also cautions preachers to develop a sense of timing that avoids dragging out homilies with anecdotes or other details that bog down the message. As a model of good timing, he cites Moses' song to the Israelites: "May my instruction soak in like the rain..."(Deuteronomy 32:2). "Too slow is ineffective and deadly; too fast is like a downpour on parched earth, so much runs off without a chance to soak in."[2] How long should a daily homily be? Two to three minutes is a typical length. Moses' image of the word as rain offers a practical guideline for the length of daily homilies. Preach a brief word that refreshes and enlivens the hearers, but does not drown them.

Celebrating the Saints

How should preachers handle the homily on feasts and memorials of saints? Do they preach about the saint's life or do they preach from the readings? For most memorials of saints, the liturgy calls for the readings from the ordinary cycle. A direct connection between the saint and the scriptures of the day is purely coincidental. Charles Miller offers a helpful guideline. He advises preachers to remember that the essence of preaching is to preach the person of Jesus Christ. Individual saints manifest a unique aspect of discipleship to Christ.[3] For example, preachers do not give a homily on the life of St. Vincent de Paul. Rather, they preach Christ whom Vincent saw in the faces of the poor.

Sample Weekday Homily

In the first reading (Exodus 3:1-6, 9-12) God appears to Moses in the burning bush and commissions Moses to be a prophet. Moses objects, "Who am I that I should go to Pharaoh?" God in turn promises, "I will be with you." In the gospel (Matthew 11:25-27) Jesus praises his Father for revealing to the merest children what God has hidden from the learned and clever.

[Moses as Every Man] The ancient Greek theater featured the character "Every Man." This "Every Person," as we might call the character today, voiced the questions and thoughts of those watching the drama. If the Greeks had produced this reading from Exodus, Moses would have made a good "Every Person." He speaks the thoughts that most of us have when we hear the Lord calling us to a difficult task. "Why me? I cannot do this work you are asking of me, Lord." Many prophets said much the same thing. Once they came to know the mind and will of God, they feared the call to speak that message to others.

[Reluctant Ministers] I have heard some ministers, both priests and sisters, who have said they could identify with a Moses who was not up to the task of confronting the Pharaoh. A friend of mine, who is a very dynamic preacher, once commented, "I feel like such a phony sometimes. I don't live half of what I talk about in homilies." Students who are just learning to preach sometimes feel very timid about speaking God's message forcefully. They know that they themselves are weak people with their own faults. We ministers sometimes become anxious because we forget who is really in charge. It is the Lord who makes our efforts bear fruit.

[Who Is Really Driving?] When I was four years old, my father took my brother and me for a drive. We went out on a country road where Dad let my older brother steer the car for a mile or so. My brother thought that was just great fun. So, of course, I asked Dad if I could drive, too. Remember, I was only four. Dad put me on his lap, put my hands up on the wheel, and down the road we went. I was convinced that I was driving the car. I did not look down to see Dad's hands on the bottom of the wheel doing the steering. That memory helps me appreciate my relationship with the Lord. Any good done in my ministry is the result of the Lord's power.

[I Will Be With You] This message is not just for ministers. Have not we all felt overwhelmed at times? Have not we all wondered where we will find the strength to do what the Lord is asking of us? Some parents have wondered where they will find the strength to raise a good family. Some grandparents have told me they feel they should do more to encourage their grandchildren to return to the church. Others face serious illness and all the stress that comes with it. At all those times, it is especially important to remember that the Lord is our strength. When we feel as if we just cannot do what the Lord is calling us to do, he is with us. Those are important times to remember what God promised to Moses when Moses objected that he was not up to the awesome task. God assured him, "I will be with you."

[Eucharist] We come to this Eucharist as the little ones Jesus calls us to be in today's gospel. In receiving this food, we express our trust that the Lord is with us. May the Lord give us the strength to be confident disciples in our daily lives.

2. Preaching at Funerals and Weddings

Funerals and weddings also present special challenges for preachers. This brief section does not present a thorough discussion of homilies preached at these special occasions. It does offer a few practical guidelines intended to stimulate a preacher's reflection.

Linking the Scriptures and the Sacraments

Funerals, weddings, baptisms and other celebrations of milestones in people's lives challenge preachers to point out links. How do the lives of those who celebrate these events connect with the scriptures proclaimed at the liturgy? As noted throughout this book, all homilies preach the person of Jesus Christ. Homilies do not preach on the mystery of death and eternal life, nor do they preach on the union of husband and wife in marriage. Funeral homilies preach Christ experienced in the lives of the community gathered for the particular person who has died. Wedding homilies preach Christ who joins this man and this woman in the sacrament of matrimony.

Attending to Emotions

People attending a funeral, for example, arrive with a mixture of emotions. Those who loved the deceased feel grief, of course. Some may also feel anger that their loved one is gone. Others may feel a sense of relief that the lengthy suffering of the deceased is finally over. Others may attend the funeral from a sense of social obligation. These latter people probably have an entirely different range of emotions. Whatever their varied feelings, the congregation is thinking about the person whose funeral they are attending. At some point in the liturgy, most people begin to reflect on their own mortality. They realize that someday people will gather for *their* funeral. How do the scriptures speak to those strong feelings? How does God's word console and offer hope? Preachers face the challenge of meeting the congregation where they are in celebrating these special times of the faith journey. Preachers announce the word that strengthens pilgrims to continue the journey with hope.

Reaching Out to Other Traditions and the Unchurched

Preaching at special occasions also offers an opportunity to reach out to believers of other traditions and to the unchurched. Nearly all in the Sunday congregation are members of the same believing tradition. Catholics worship in Catholic churches, Presbyterians worship in Presbyterian churches. Funerals, weddings, baptisms and other special occasions present a different situation. Friends, acquaintances and coworkers who attend these events come from a variety of Christian and non-Christian traditions. Some may attend no church or synagogue. Preachers cannot assume that everyone in the congregation will appreciate allusions to scripture passages or practices of the tradition. Homilies at these special events can include a few words of welcome and a sensitivity to those who may not understand what our own tradition believes.

At the wedding of a Catholic couple who was very involved in a lay ministry, seven priests with whom the bride and groom had worked concelebrated at the liturgy. A Protestant in the congregation later remarked to the presider, "It surprised me to see your weddings involve so many ministers. We just have one minister at a wedding in our church." A preacher who is sensitive to these visitors could have explained the presence of the concelebrating clergy.

3. Funeral Homilies

The *Order of Christian Funerals* provides the following description of funeral homilies:

> A brief homily based on the readings is always given after the gospel reading at the funeral liturgy and may also be given after the readings at the vigil service; but there is never to be a eulogy. Attentive to the grief of those present, the homilist should dwell on God's compassionate love and on the paschal mystery of the Lord, as proclaimed in the Scripture readings" (*Order of Christian Funerals* General Introduction, n. 27).

Celebrating Grief

The funeral rite directs preachers to be attentive to grief in the congregation. Funeral homilies do great violence to the grieving when they suggest that tears are a sign of selfishness. Some preachers have even said, "If we truly believed in eternal life we would not be weeping, we would be rejoicing that the dead are enjoying eternal life." That may be theologically valid, but it shows no sensitivity to natural human feelings. Who more than Jesus believed in eternal life? Yet, when he stood at the tomb of his dead friend Lazarus, Jesus wept. Tears do not show a lack of faith. They show deep love. The congregation has a right to their grief.

Being Personal

For believers, grief is not the whole story. There is also the story of how Christ has been alive in the individual who has died. The rite also reminds preachers that funeral homilies are not eulogies. These tributes, which have their origin in the classical Greek *"panegyric,"* praise the lives and accomplishments of the deceased who are now gone forever. Nothing remains but to remember those who once lived among us.

Believers gather not just to remember the dead, but to celebrate the mystery of new life in Christ who has conquered the power of death. Family and friends have not gathered just to reflect on eternal life as a theological abstraction. Believers celebrate the Christian death of particular individuals. Funeral homilies that are sensitive to the congregation avoid generalities; they speak in very specific and personal language.[4]

When Preachers Do Not Know the Deceased

Preachers can make a funeral homily personal even when they have had no contact with the deceased. Charles Hudson suggests that preachers meet with family members to listen to their stories. At that time, the preacher might begin by saying, "I did not have the pleasure of knowing Elizabeth, but I would like to hear more about her." Most people open up to that type of invitation and speak very freely. Hudson suggests preachers ask specific questions about what the deceased enjoyed doing, their deep values, or any accomplishments in which they took special pride. One helpful question is, "If they wished to leave one last thought for those attending this funeral service, what do you think it would be?"[5]

Being True to Theology

At times, preachers preside at funerals for persons who did not evidence any real desire to live as a Christian. Alvin Rueter cautions preachers to be true to theology. God who gives persons free will does not force love on anyone. Jesus spoke of separating sheep from goats at the final judgment. In funerals of those who showed little commitment to Christ, Rueter counsels preachers to offer comfort to those experiencing loss by "putting their dear one in the best possible light."[6] Funeral homilies, as the rite says, minister to the living, not to the dead.

4. Sample Funeral Homily

The congregation is comprised of the family and friends of Lawrence, a 65-year-old man who died after several years of battling cancer. The first reading is from the Book of Wisdom (3:1-9): "The souls of the just are in the hand of God...." The second is from Romans (6:3-9): "If, then, we have died with Christ, we believe that we shall also live with him." The gospel reading is from John (11:32-45): Jesus raises Lazarus from the dead.

> [Jesus Wept] Marjorie, and Thomas, Louise and Henry, I want to assure you that you are not alone in your sorrow. You do not stand alone as you mourn your husband and father. Many of your friends stood with you at the funeral home yesterday. Others are here today. As we just heard in this gospel, another person stands with you in this time of sorrow. That person is Jesus himself. Jesus who believed in eternal life, Jesus who preached about the joys of heaven, wept at the death of Lazarus. Those who believe in eternal life still have a right to feel great sadness today. Our tears are good. The bystanders at the tomb of Lazarus had it right when they saw Jesus weeping. They said among themselves that Jesus must have loved Lazarus very much to be weeping so deeply. That is what our grief says to us. Our tears tell us how deeply we loved Lawrence. Jesus felt that same depth of sadness. He showed it in his own tears.
>
> [Jesus Raises Lazarus] While it is comforting for us to know that Jesus understands our grief, the gospel shows us that sadness is not the end of the story. What happened next is the most important part of this gospel. Jesus brought his friend Lazarus back to life. Jesus has power to turn death into new life. In that very dramatic moment, Jesus showed us that death is not the end of the

story. As the Book of Wisdom told us, to our unaided human eyes the dead seem to be gone forever. They seem to have suffered a great tragedy. We believers know the truth—Jesus raises the dead to new life.

[Our Lady of the Snows] Saturday night I decided to take a walk at the Shrine of Our Lady of the Snows. In all the years I have lived in our area, I had never visited that shrine. For some reason, I decided to go there Saturday. Within a few minutes of starting my walk, I came upon the Wall of the Fathers, a prayer wall containing hundreds of names of deceased fathers. It dawned on me that the following day was Father's Day. I started thinking about my dad who died several years ago, and began to feel great sadness. An old wound opened up again. Just as I was steeped in my own grief, I came upon the Garden of Resurrection. In this garden there is a model of the tomb where they laid Jesus. At the back of the empty tomb a bright flame burns. An inscription in stone reminds us that Jesus is no longer here, because he is risen. My walk around the shrine put me in touch with many images of death and new life. It turned out to be something of a field trip. I remembered how the end of our earthly life is not really the end. Our death is the beginning of what the Lord promised all of us when he raised Lazarus. We are a people called to new, everlasting life.

[We Are Baptized into Christ's Death and Resurrection] Paul reminds us that new life began at our baptism. We were baptized into the death and resurrection of Christ. At the start of this Mass we covered the casket with a white cloth as a reminder of Lawrence's baptism. This was no mere ceremonial gesture, but an expression of the profound act that changed us forever at our baptism. Our baptism is really the first step in our lifelong journey to eternal life.

The early Christians celebrated baptism in a way that made it clear they saw it as the place where death and new life come together. When adults wished baptism in the ancient church they walked to the door of the church and stopped at the edge of the baptismal pool. They took off their outer garments as a sign they were throwing off the old sinful life they had known. They walked down stone steps into the water and were completely submerged. This was a spiritual death, a baptism into the death of Christ. They then walked up the steps on the other side of the pool and were admitted into the church. The minister clothed them in a long white robe as a sign that they were now a new creation, baptized into Christ's resurrection. Even if we celebrate baptism differently today, the reality of what happens to us is the same. We become a new creation. Despite all our human weaknesses and faults, baptism changes us into people whom the Lord calls to eternal life.

[Lawrence Is in Good Hands] You and I, along with Lawrence, started our lives claimed for Christ at our baptism. We await the time in the future when Christ calls us too, to eternal life. God's word from the Book of Wisdom assures us that "The souls of the just are in the hand of God." Although we may weep as Jesus did at the tomb of Lazarus, may we also find strength that Lawrence and all of us are in good hands.

5. Wedding Homilies

What Wedding and Funeral Preaching Have in Common

Weddings and funerals share many of the same opportunities and challenges for preachers. As already noted, both events involve linking the scriptures with the special occasion. Both also offer the chance for outreach to other traditions and the unchurched. Hudson's suggestion that preachers meet with the family of the deceased is also appropriate for weddings. Although preachers will become acquainted with the couple during the wedding preparation, they may also find it helpful to talk with the bride and groom's families. The marriage rite, like the funeral rite, gives directives on the content of the wedding homily. It calls for preachers to be mindful of "the circumstances of this particular marriage."[7]

Wedding homilies, like all homilies, move beyond theological abstractions. The congregation has gathered to celebrate the marriage of a particular couple. The parents of the groom (we will call him Tom Smith) told the preacher about the day their seven-year-old son came home and announced, "Mom and Dad, someday I'm going to marry Sally Jones." Later that day the Smiths told their neighbors what their son had confided. The Joneses laughed as they reported how Sally had come home that same afternoon to tell them, "Mom and Dad, I don't like that old Tom Smith!" The preacher had a ready-made introduction for the wedding homily.

6. Sample Wedding Homily

The congregation consists of the family and friends of Scott and Denise. The first reading is from 1 Corinthians (12:31-13:8) in which Paul describes true love. It is patient, kind, never jealous. The second is from Mathew (22:35-40): Jesus gives the two great commandments, to love God and our neighbor.

> [A Perfect Wedding Day] Scott and Denise told me last night that they were hoping for a perfect wedding day. I think they have succeeded so far. Denise looks lovely in her elegant wedding dress. Scott looks handsome in his tuxedo. The wedding party looks as if they could be in a movie. As I look in the faces of the family and friends, I see pride and joy. Long months of planning have come together this day. Everything is just about perfect, as we hope it would be on a wedding day.
>
> [Marriage Involves Challenges] I would love to tell you, Scott and Denise, that every day of your marriage is going to be just as delightful as this day is. Married couples who are here today know that is not so. Even the best marriage faces struggles and difficulties in real life. Successful marriages result when couples face challenges together and work at building their relationship. Building a committed relationship takes time.
>
> [Stages of Commitment] When any of us commit to another person, or to a community, we go through several stages. In the first stage, we often wear rose-colored glasses. We are in love with the person, or thrilled to

belong to the new community. Things could not be sweeter. This is the stage of romantic songs and poetry. In the second stage, we remove those rose colored glasses and begin to notice reality. We can begin to feel disillusioned or disappointed at what we suddenly start to notice. Our partner, or the community we have joined, does not appear as perfect as they once did. The third stage, which is the most important one, involves our choice. We decide that we want to work at the commitment, in good times and bad.

I have not experienced married commitment, of course, but I do know what it means to be committed as a priest. Priesthood and marriage have the same elements. Both are lifelong commitments. My ordination day was just as perfect as this wedding is today. My family and friends filled the church. The same atmosphere of joy we feel now permeated my ordination ceremony. Within a few months, I entered that second stage where I began to face some challenges that go with being a priest. I thank God I made it to the present stage where I am choosing to work at the commitment. It takes a great deal of love to make a marriage or any serious commitment succeed.

[Genuine Love] Scott and Denise chose a reading about this type of love. Paul, the apostle, tells us what real love is about. Love is not the trivial emotion we sometimes hear reflected in romantic songs and movies. Real love, which Paul is talking about, allows us to work at relationships and commitments. Genuine love is patient, kind, knows no limits when it comes to trust and hope. Love is not jealous, rude or snobbish. Love does not brood over injuries. Scott and Denise, when you begin to face challenges in your marriage, as you surely will, I hope you recall this reading you chose for your wedding day.

[The Great Commandments] You chose a gospel that also speaks about genuine love. Jesus takes Paul's praise of love further by commanding that we love one another. Can anyone really command us to love? I doubt that

Scott or Denise need a command to love today, but there will be days when this command to love may be necessary. What will happen when Scott throws his dirty socks on the floor once too often? Or how about when Denise wants to go out with her friends instead of staying home to watch the Chicago Bears play football on television? These are times when both must choose what it means to love. They may need to remember that Jesus commands us to love.

[Scott and Denise Are the Ministers] This wedding is a first step that Scott and Denise are taking in response to Jesus' call to love. I am not the minister of this sacrament. Although I have an official role in the ceremony, the couple are the ministers. Except when administering baptism in extraordinary circumstances, marriage is the only sacrament where laypersons are the ministers. In this sacrament, a man and a woman commit themselves to one another. Because this is a sacrament, the Lord becomes a partner in that commitment. Scott and Denise, in taking one another today, you are asking that the Lord bless your union. Rely on Jesus to be the strength of your marriage.

[We Are With You] A wise person once observed, "A beautiful young couple in love is nothing unusual. We can find them everywhere. A beautiful old couple in love is something else. They are a lifelong work of art." If everyone in this church could stand up here and talk to you right now, Scott and Denise, I am sure they would all tell you much the same thing. They would tell you that they rejoice with you, and they pray for you as you begin a lifetime of discovering how to become a beautiful old couple.

7. Preaching to Children

"Let the Children Come to Me..."

Preaching to children, like all preaching, begins by exegeting the congregation. Who are these little people squirming in the pews? What do they think of God? Do they consider Jesus their friend or just another mysterious grownup? The gospel shows us one group of children who found Jesus very welcoming. Teachers and other professionals who work with children have much to offer preachers about how to open the scriptures for little ones.

A preacher told of his visit to a widow's home the day her husband died after a long illness. Her family had gathered at the house to wait with her during the last days of her husband's life. Her pastor had been preparing the funeral homily, but knew that it was missing something. He did not know what. As the priest was talking with the man's wife about the funeral service, the four-year-old granddaughter walked into the room. She came up to the priest and said, "Grandpa became an angel today." That was the missing element for the homily. Children have profound insights to offer preachers.

Honesty with Children

Children speak to grownups in simple and direct language. Preachers need to speak simply and directly to children. Adults often develop sophisticated verbal skills that subtly mask true beliefs and feelings. Children deserve honesty from preachers. Francis Cancro advises preachers to let children know that they themselves are pilgrims along with the children. The only difference is that preachers have been walking the road longer than the children.[8] If the gospel for the day presents Jesus calling us to love God with our whole minds and hearts, for example, preachers could talk about their own struggle finding time to pray. Children, just beginning to learn how to interact with others, know what it means to be misunderstood. How refreshing it would be for them to hear that preachers sometimes try to do their best, but others don't appreciate or understand their efforts. Adults have a responsibility to teach and guide young people, but that does not mean adults know all the answers. Pilgrims of all ages can travel together along the road as disciples.

Witnessing to Children

Children may not understand every word preachers use, but they will hear how preachers feel about God by the way they speak. I have a vivid memory of a phrase used in a homily I heard when I was about ten years of age. The priest wanted to express that he was sixty years old. He did not say, "I am sixty." He said with a deep sigh, "In my sixty years in this vale of tears called life...." I do not remember the rest of the homily. My young mind did not go beyond that one very telling phrase, delivered by a man who did not sound as if he were enjoying his discipleship.

Our tone of voice says a great deal about who we are and how we feel about being a follower of Jesus. Homilies go beyond telling children about God; they tell children how the adult preachers feel about their faith. Will children hear that faith in God is life-giving, or will they hear that religion is a burden to be endured? This does not mean that preachers present their faith as one cheery moment of bliss after another. Children, and the rest of us, deserve honesty. Children experience struggles that can range from having their pet run away to having their parents divorce. Some know addiction in their families. Others have had to deal with the death of a close friend or family member. They need to hear preachers who can express the good news that God is with us in all these difficulties. Disciples live in hope, especially in the face of great challenges.

Resources for Preaching to Children

The director of religious education in a local parish can be a valuable resource for helping ministers develop skills in preaching to children. Preachers could plan homilies with the director and ask for feedback after preaching the homily.

If ministers decide that they are not ready to preach to children, they can invite the director of religious education or another qualified person to preach at the children's liturgy. The *Directory for Masses With Children offers this option. (Introduction to the Roman Missal*, n. 24).

8. Sample Children's Homily

The liturgical celebration is the feast of the Dedication of the Lateran Basilica; the gospel for the occasion is the call of Zacchaeus (Luke 19:1-10).

[Judging Others Unfairly] Many years ago, before I studied to be a priest, I worked at an office in Chicago. My office was in a poor part of the city. There were many homeless men and women in that neighborhood. I got to know some of them because they would ask me for money. A man I enjoyed talking with called himself Spider. One day Spider asked me for fifty cents. He promised he would pay me back in a few days. I gave him the money, but I did not think I would ever get it back. However, in just a few days Spider returned the fifty cents. A few weeks later he asked for a dollar, again promising that he would pay me back. He did give me back the dollar. Another office worker warned me, "Be careful, Spider is getting ready to trick you. He will make you think you can trust him and then he will borrow a lot of money and not repay it." One week later, Spider asked to borrow twenty dollars. Back in those days that was a lot of money, but I gave him the money, thinking I would never see it again. I did not see Spider for a long time. I decided the other office worker was correct: Spider was just a cheat who had tricked me.

Many weeks later, Spider came running down the street toward me. When he caught up with me, he said, "I've been looking for you everywhere. I owe you this twenty dollars and thought I might not find you again. Here it is." I judged Spider unfairly. I had thought he was a cheat, but he was a very honest person. The gospel tells us today about another person, Zacchaeus, whom people judged unfairly.

[Tax Collectors and the Rich] Zacchaeus was a chief tax collector and a very rich man. That is why people judged him unfairly. In Jesus' time, people were very suspicious of the rich. There was only so much wealth to go around. If someone was rich, they probably got their wealth by taking what belonged to others. If Jonathan owned two mules, it was because poor Esau had no mules. Because Zacchaeus was very rich, people decided he was a no-good sinner. The gospel tells us that Zacchaeus was really a good man.

[Jesus Meets Zacchaeus] When Jesus came to his town, Zacchaeus really wanted to get a good look at him. Since Zacchaeus was a short person, he could not see over the crowd. Some of you probably know what that is like. Did you ever go to a movie when a tall man or woman sat in front of you and you could not see around them? That was the same problem Zacchaeus faced when he wanted to see Jesus. So he climbed up a tall tree to get a good look. That extra effort made a big impression on Jesus. Jesus called Zacchaeus down out of the tree and went to his house for dinner. The story tells us more about people judging others unfairly. The people were shocked that Jesus would have anything to do with this sinner. The people not only judged Zacchaeus, they judged Jesus.

Jesus looked at Zacchaeus differently than the crowd did. Jesus saw the good in Zacchaeus. When Jesus and Zacchaeus met at the house, Zacchaeus agreed to give away half of his money to the poor. He added that if he cheated anyone, he would pay them back four times as much. Jesus was pleased at this desire to live a good life. Jesus proclaims that this is what it means to be part of God's family.

[Church as a Place of Healing] This story shows us how Jesus treats us as members of his family, the church. Jesus forgives us and welcomes us back when we stray from God. Today, church members all over the world honor St. John Lateran, a church building in Rome. Why would we be honoring a church building in a far-off country? Actually we are not just honoring a building of stone. We are celebrating the fact that we are God's people, the living church.

[At This Eucharist, Jesus Feeds His Family] At this Eucharist we will see this gospel story lived out here in our own church. Jesus and Zacchaeus probably sat down together to eat a meal. That is what people did when they visited someone's house. Jesus invites us to the meal of his body and blood in this Eucharist. Let us come to this meal happy that Jesus invites us to be in his family.

Further Reading

Daily Homilies

Rueter, Alvin. *Making Good Preaching Better: A Step-by-Step Guide to Scripture-Based, People-Centered Preaching.* Collegeville, Minn.: Liturgical Press, 1997. Rueter employs a practical, step-by-step approach to teaching preaching. Although his is a textbook for seminarians, experienced preachers will find helpful insights. Chapter Nine, on creativity, can help preachers develop a habit of homily preparation for weekday preaching.

Children's Books

Olszewski, Darl. B*alloons! Candy! Toys!: And Other Parables for Storytellers.* San Jose, Calif.: Resource Publications, 1986. Olszewski presents a series of stories that speak to the world of children. After each story, he provides strategies for helping children apply the stories to their own faith journey.

Pfister, Marcus. *The Rainbow Fish.* New York: North South Books, 1996. The Rainbow Fish learns what it means to share.

Roche, Luane. *The Proud Tree.* Ligouri, Mo.: Ligouri, 1997. The personified tree, whose wood made the cross of Jesus, describes the crucifixion.

Wood, Douglas. *Old Turtle.* Illustrated by Cheng-Khee Chee. Duluth, Minn.: Pfeifer-Ha, 1991. The story takes place in an ancient time before humans. The animals argue about what God is like. The character, Old Turtle, describes God as many-faceted.

Notes

1. Edward Fischer, *Everybody Steals from God* (Notre Dame, Ind.: University of Notre Dame Press, 1977), pp. 33-34.

2. Fischer, p.103.

3. Charles Miller, *Ordained to Preach* (New York: Alba House 1992), p. 161.

4. William A. Richard, "The Funeral Homily: Personal, but Not a Eulogy," *Church*, Summer (1992): 18.

5. Charles Hudson, "Preaching to the Living at a Funeral," in *Preaching Better*, ed. Frank J. McNulty (New York: Paulist Press,

1985), p. 119.

6. Alvin C. Rueter, Making Good *Preaching Better: A Step-by-Step Guide to Scripture-Based, People-Centered Preaching* (Collegeville, Minn.: Liturgical Press, 1997), p. 182.

7. "Rite of Marriage," in *The Rites of the Catholic Church*, trans. International Commission on English in the Liturgy (New York: Pueblo, 1976), n. 22.

8. Francis T. Cancro, "To Live the Word with Little Folks," in *Preaching Better*, ed. Frank J. McNulty (New York: Paulist Press, 1985), p. 101.

Using This Book with Groups

1. Session Components

This appendix describes in detail how a group can organize and use the sessions of *We Speak the Word of the Lord*. The process involves these four elements, described in the following paragraphs: the group composed of preachers gathered for peer learning, the contents of this book, homilies preached by the participants, and video resources.

A. *The Group*
Group members are the primary component. Ultimately, using this book for continuing formation and education will succeed only to the extent that the preachers themselves choose to make it work. The leader, chosen by the group, does not direct the learning. In this peer-learning setting, leaders are not expected to be professionally trained in homiletics. Leaders are responsible only for facilitating the group's process.

B. *This Book*
This book is divided into eight chapters that explore various facets of preaching. Each group session, based on one of the chapters, offers questions and issues for group discussion, a workshop activity, and a suggested assignment for the next group meeting. Groups can design a preaching program that fits the members' particular needs. Some groups may choose to follow the book in its entirety; others may decide to use only some chapters. The chapters can be used in any order, except for Chapter One, which is foundational for a group's subsequent work. All groups should begin with this chapter.

C. *Homilies by Group Members*
The program, as outlined in this appendix, suggests that groups alternate discussion sessions with preaching sessions. Homilies can be recorded on audiotape or videotape as they are actually preached at the liturgy. Group members may then comment on each homily.

D. Video Resources

For some sessions, group members may wish to discuss audio-tapes or videotapes of their own homilies or of professionally recorded examples of preaching provided by local resource centers.

2. Homily Tapes

One of the clearest ways ministers can discover how congregations hear them is to observe their preaching on tape. Groups will face several practical considerations when using these tapes in the sessions.

Video or Audio?

Videotapes provide a fuller experience than audiotapes do in that they enable others to view gestures and facial expressions that are an important part of the preaching event. Whether groups choose videotape or audiotape will usually depend upon their method of distributing homily tapes to other group members.

Distributing Tapes to Other Group Members

If group members decide to hear the homilies for the first time in the group session, there should be no difficulty in recording them on videotape. However, some groups may find it helpful to have tapes of every homily a few days before the session meets. In this case, audiotapes would be the more practical choice.

Getting a Clear Recording

Preachers may need to experiment with recording techniques to ensure a clear recording. If others find themselves straining to listen to a tape, it may color their perception of the homily. An excellent message that can barely be heard forces the listeners to expend undue energy trying to determine what the preacher is saying. In some cases, a recorder can be connected directly to the sound system. If that is not possible, preachers can place a small recorder on the pulpit. If preachers do not use the pulpit, they may try placing a small dictation recorder in their pocket. In this case, they should use a lapel microphone to ensure a clear recording.

Homily Texts

Groups may decide that a written homily text (or detailed outline) would aid them in providing feedback to one another. These texts can help listeners refer to specific areas of the homily when making observations. Some groups supply transcripts taken from the homily tapes. Or, it may be helpful to see the text as it was written before the homily was preached. This helps others see how preachers edited the message during the actual preaching. Preachers would be expected to append a brief analysis of the congregation to the homily text or outline. These analyses contain a description of the listeners and the preaching situation, along with the specific purpose of the homily being discussed.

Length of the Homily

Group members will listen to and comment on a number of homilies during the review sessions. To keep the sessions from becoming too long, it is important to limit homilies to a maximum of ten minutes.

3. Organizing a Group

As already mentioned, the group members are the most important components of this program. These guidelines are helpful in establishing the group and choosing the group leader.

Group Size

Groups will vary in size but certain minimum and maximum limits are important to consider. On the one hand, groups that are too small will not allow the level of dynamic interaction that makes for lively discussion. On the other, if groups are too large, it can be difficult for all members to participate in discussion and workshop activities. This program is designed for groups between five and ten members.

It will be necessary to divide a large group into smaller sections when preachers meet for homily feedback sessions. A small group of five or six persons will require a minimum of two hours to hear and comment on the homilies. A large group may therefore decide to meet as one group when they discuss topics and participate in workshop activities, and to gather in small groups when they offer feedback on the homilies. Another option might be to always meet as a large group. In this case, half of the group presents tapes of their homilies at one session, while the others present tapes at the next session.

Group Membership

The most important criterion for deciding who will compose a group is whether the members can work well together. Preachers may not necessarily agree with one another on many issues, but they will be expected to care about one another's progress by offering honest feedback.

Priests, deacons and lay preachers may wish to form groups made up only of preachers from their own vocational states. A clear advantage to this type of group is that all members share common experiences and challenges. In other cases, groups may find it enriching to be composed of preachers from all three groups. Some groups may also wish to include preachers from other Christian traditions.   Whatever the path a group takes, it would be wise to have periodic self-evaluations and be willing to make whatever adjustments might be necessary. The important thing is that people find themselves in a group where they can work with others on the ministry of preaching.

Choosing a Group Leader

It is presumed that group leaders will not be trained homiletics teachers, but they will need expertise in organizing a peer-learning group. The sessions present options for how groups can deal with certain topics and book chapters. The taped homilies, for example, can be handled in a variety of ways. In addition, groups need to choose the dates and times of their meetings. Because group leaders help organize the decision making for these and other details, groups will want to choose their leaders carefully. The position should not simply default to the person willing to take on the role.

Video Resources

Groups are encouraged to seek out additional video, audio and print resources to supplement this book. Some dioceses maintain learning resource centers that can provide these materials. Videotapes that feature model homilies can be especially helpful in the early stages of a group's work together. Most people find it less threatening to critique a homily from a preacher who is not a member of the peer-learning group.

4. Sample Group Session

Groups that choose to follow the program in its entirety will convene approximately twenty times. They may meet every two weeks or once a month. Half the meetings will be devoted to discussing the eight chapters of this book (Discussion Sessions); the rest will be devoted to giving feedback on one another's homilies (Homily Sessions). This section describes both types of meetings.

Discussion Sessions

Input:
Participants prepare for a meeting by reading one of the book chapters. The first chapter, What Is a Homily?, for example, provides a brief history of the liturgical homily before and after the Second Vatican Council. It also explores the major issues in determining the nature and purpose of the homily.

Discussion:
The discussion section of each session contains specific questions and issues to guide the group's discussion. The group may propose its own issues for discussion in light of their particular needs.

Activity:
After the discussion, there is an activity that allows group members to apply the material to concrete preaching situations. At some sessions, for example, groups may view a homily on videotape and critique it in light of the topic they have discussed. Most sessions conclude with a suggested specific assignment for the next meeting. These assignments usually involve some aspect of the homily that the participants will prepare for the next session. Discussion Sessions alternate with Homily Sessions.

Homily Sessions

The alternate type of meeting is one at which group members critique homilies of other members. It is vital that preachers agree to participate in these sessions with a spirit of openness and honesty. If groups follow the norms described below, they will create an atmosphere that will facilitate the success of the peer-learning process. Participants may wish to discuss these five norms, and even amend them or add new ones, provided all participants agree with the changes.

1. Participate as fully as possible. Group members agree to participate in the feedback sessions to the best of their ability. They agree that the success of this peer learning experience depends on the efforts of each group member to encourage the development of each other as preachers.

2. Critique the homily, not the preacher. Participants agree to critique homilies, not the preachers. It is true that homilies are windows to the personal faith of preachers, revealing a great deal about what the preachers know, believe and value. Nevertheless, the group's homilies are the focus of discussion, not the preachers themselves.

3. Be supportive in calling preachers to growth. Honest feedback often involves pointing out areas where homilies need improvement. Preachers agree to be supportive, especially when calling others to further growth. Whenever possible, participants will offer suggestions for improving a homily rather than simply pointing out its faults.

4. Observe the time limits. Group members will limit the length of their preaching so that all homilies can be heard and critiqued within the agreed-upon period. Participants will commit themselves to spending an equal amount of time giving feedback to each preacher. Group members agree not to monopolize time.

5. Clarify expectations. Spend a few moments at the first homily session clarifying the expectations that each participant brings to the group. Respond to these questions: "Why did I join this group?" "What do I hope to learn from others?" "What do I think I can offer to others?"

The First Meeting

At their first meeting the group will find it important to decide the following housekeeping issues:

1. Choose a group leader. Although this program follows a peer learning model, a group requires a leader to facilitate the many practical details that are contribute to the group's success. In particular, the group leader facilitates scheduling and holds the group to the time limits the members agree to follow. In some cases a leader may be responsible for locating other learning resources for the group.

2. Determine a schedule of meetings. Some groups may find it necessary to schedule each individual meeting on a date and time that allows all members to be present. A regular schedule of monthly or bimonthly sessions allows for better planning. If possible, at this first session, group members agree upon a regular time for all future meetings.

3. Set time limits. Time limits are an important part of group process. In a well-run group, sessions begin and end on time. The chapters in the book lend themselves to a session of two hours, with a break in the middle. In the sessions devoted to reviewing and commenting on homilies, groups will need to set a maximum time limit to deal with each group member's homily.

4. Determine the agenda for the next meeting. The group decides the agenda for the next session.

Conclusion

The first Christian preachers were eyewitnesses. In their enthusiasm for preaching the Jesus they had known personally, they may have gathered in a group similar to the one the peer group forms. They certainly must have encouraged one another in their preaching ministry. Perhaps they even offered suggestions to one another about how their preaching could be improved. The Spirit abided with this original handful of disciples who began to preach a word that is now placed on the lips of the preacher-members. May the Spirit continue to work powerfully in those who preach God's word.

Discussion Session Guidelines

1. Chapter One: What Is a Homily?

For Reflection and Discussion

Discuss these questions from your *personal experience* as a preacher.

1. What is the difference between teaching *about* God in a homily and *preaching God?*

2. *Fulfilled in Your Hearing* says preachers do not "so much attempt to explain the Scriptures as to interpret the human situation through the Scriptures."(n. 20) What are some specific ways that preachers can get to know the human situation of the congregation?

3. What does the definition of a homily given in this chapter imply for preachers in terms of their personal prayer?

4. Discuss the following quotations in light of your personal experience of preaching.

Karl Barth on preaching the person of Christ:
> There is no wisdom in stopping at the next-to-the-last and the next-to-the-next- to-the-last want of the people; and they will not thank us for doing so. They expect us to understand them better than they understand themselves, and to take them more seriously than they take themselves ["The Need and Promise of Christian Preaching," in *The Word of God and The Word of Man* (New York: Harper, 1957), p. 109].

Raymond Brown on the preaching from the Acts of the Apostles:
> The very fact that the author [of Acts] mentions that those who accepted this proclamation were soon called Christians means that it is inconceivable that Christ is not the primary proclamation. If I may be permitted to draw from this a lesson for our proclamation today, I would insist that what God did in Jesus Christ must still be the heart of our message. That does not mean that we

can ignore implications about what we are to do toward God and toward humanity; but all such obligation of action depends on understanding and believing in Jesus Christ ["Preaching in the Acts of the Apostles," in *A New Look at Preaching*, ed. John Burke (Wilmington, Del.: Michael Glazier, 1983), pp. 64-65.]

Walter Burghardt on knowing the God we preach:

Can you say that, like Ignatius, you have truly encountered the living and true God? Can you say that you know God Himself, not simply human words that describe Him? If you cannot, I dare not conclude that you are an unproductive preacher; for the same God who "is able from these stones to raise up children to Abraham"(Mt. 3:9) can use the most sere of sermons to move the obdurate heart. But I do say that if you know only a theology of God, not the God of theology, you will not be the preacher our world desperately needs ["From Study to Proclamation," in *A New Look at Preaching*, ed. John Burke (Wilmington, Del.: Michael Glazier, 1983), p. 34.]

Activity

View the taped homily provided by the group leader. Discuss it in terms of the topic, "What Is a Homily?" The following questions can be used to guide the discussion.

1. To what extent does the preaching fit the following definition of a homily?

A homily is a preaching event that is integral to the liturgy to proclaim the saving mystery of God in the scriptures. It calls and empowers the hearers to faith, a deeper participation in the Eucharist, and daily discipleship to Christ lived out in the church.

2. Did the homily teach *about* God or preach God?

3. How did the preacher handle any issues that called for instruction? Was there too much explanation, or not enough to help the proclamation?

4. Was there good news in the homily for you? Describe what it was.

5. What is the one most important thing the preacher could do to make this homily better?

For Next Time
In the next session, participants will offer feedback to one another based on the tapes of their homilies. Use the questions from the Activity section above to guide the next session.

2. Chapter Two: What Makes a Homily Outstanding?

For Reflection and Discussion
Discuss how the Christmas homily in this chapter (pp. 40-43) does or does not meet each of the eight qualities of outstanding homilies.

1. Does the homily simply tell the listener what the scripture text is about, or does it help the listener interact with the various moves in the scripture text? Cite particular homily moves in support of your comments.

2. Does the preacher seem to be speaking from personal faith experience? What is the role of personal faith experience in preparing a homily? What is the role of explicit witness in preaching? What is the role of implicit witness?

3. How does the homily use concrete images to help communicate the message? What other images, instances or stories would help you appreciate the central idea?

4. Is this homily in touch with the listeners' lives? Which homily moves deal with faith life experiences? What other real life issues might the preacher have talked about in light of the central idea?

5. What inductive strategies are used in this homily? Open system preaching attempts to engage the listeners' active participation. What sections of the homily employ open-system preaching?

6. How would you express the central idea of this homily?

7. How did the preacher keep the language clear and simple?

8. Now use these questions for a homily that you have recently preached or heard.

Activity
Finding Moves in the Scriptures: Using the following blank

boxes, record in the boxes provided each move in the gospel for next Sunday, as was demonstrated in Chapter Two on pages 37-39. When finished, consider the questions that follow.

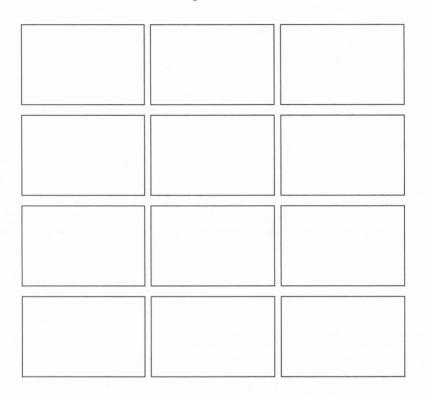

1. Which of these moves best gets to the heart of the matter in the reading?

2. Which move is the appropriate starting point for a homily in light of your particular congregation? Why?

3. Are there any moves you would probably not deal with in the homily? Why would you not include them?

4. Would you begin with a different move if you were preaching in any of the following situations?
  • Preaching to children
  • Preaching to teenagers
  • A Eucharist at which a baptism will be celebrated
  • A Sunday when couples renew wedding vows
  • Any other special situation in your congregation

For Next Time

After deciding which move from the reading is the best starting point for a homily, arrange the rest of the scripture moves in the order that you would deal with them in a homily. Construct your next homily in moves that include each of the scripture moves on which you will preach.

3. Chapter Three: Creating a Homily

For Reflection and Discussion

Consider these issues from your experience of preparing homilies.

1. Describe in detail how you prepare a homily.

2. Are there any special preparation techniques that you use frequently?

3. Have you found any advantage in starting to prepare a homily early in the week?

4. Brewster Ghiselin observes that creative people usually allow time for ideas or projects to gestate. Have you found it helpful to leave the preparation process for a time and return to it later?

5. Do you ever use published homily helps or services? Which ones? Describe how you use them.

6. Do you ever work with others in preparing a homily? If so, describe the process.

Activity

Choose at least one of the following workshop activities. Your group may wish to schedule the other options for later meetings.

1. Ask one group member to prepare background material on next Sunday's readings. As a group, brainstorm on a major theme from the readings; narrow the brainstorm list; decide on one central idea. Discuss any other issues that would help proclaim the word in a creative way. Allow at least one hour for the entire process.

2. Someone will read the gospel aloud for the following Sunday. The volunteer then assumes a character from that gospel or the character of someone standing by, watching the speech or action in the gospel. After allowing a short time for "getting into the scene,"

the volunteer describes the sights, sounds, feelings and anything else that happened during the experience of imagining. Discuss how the process might influence composing a homily on this gospel.

3. One diocese has a professional journalist edit the written homily texts for preachers in a homily study group. Consider inviting a journalist (perhaps from the diocesan newspaper) to comment on the group's homilies. The edited texts might be shared with the entire group as a learning experience.

4. Discuss how the gospel for next Sunday could be preached using a creative form. For example, could the homily, or part of the homily, be written and read as a letter to someone? Could part of the homily be acted out in a brief drama? Perhaps the homily might begin from a "what if" point of view. That is, what if this part of the gospel did not exist? How would life be different? How is life affected because this gospel does exist? These are only sample forms. What others can the group name?

For Next Time

In giving feedback during the next round of homilies, emphasize the use of creativity. Try to suggest at least one creative, fresh alternative to the approach each preacher took in writing the homily.

4. Chapter Four: Preaching the Scriptures

For Reflection and Discussion

The group will not be able to adequately deal with the For Reflection and Discussion as well as the Activity sections at one meeting. If group members decide to engage in the Activity exercise at a later meeting, they may choose to discuss the following questions at this session.

1. Charles Bouchard writes, "Every scriptural passage, because it is the word of God, has within it the potential to illumine any topic"("Authentic Preaching on Moral Issues," in *In the Company of Preachers*, p. 197). Do you agree or disagree? Why?

2. Read the story of the Prodigal Son (Luke 15:11-31). How might this passage illumine a homily that deals with abortion? Concern for the poor? Fair housing? Ethics in the workplace?

3. Discuss the published resources (print, Internet, etc.) you find

helpful in studying the scriptures for preaching.

4. What criteria do you use to decide which results of your scripture research belong in the homily and which do not?

5. What are the advantages and disadvantages of reading published homilies while preparing to preach?

6. Describe the steps you use in moving from the readings to a homily.

7. How might members of the congregation be included in studying and discussing next Sunday's readings?

Activity

Begin to prepare one or more of the readings for next Sunday by discussing the following questions. Group members may wish to divide responsibility for researching specific questions before the session.

Historical Issues

1. Who wrote this text? When? Why?

2. Do these issues have consequences for the homily?

3. What is the context of this passage within its own book of the Bible?

4. Does the context of the passage influence how it might be interpreted? If so, how?

Literary Issues

1. What is the literary form of this passage? Parable? Narrative? Example story? Prophecy? Epistle? Apocalyptic? History? Or another?

2. Does the form of the passage suggest its interpretation? If so, how?

3. Does the form of the passage suggest a form that could be used in constructing the homily?

Linking the Text to Listeners

1. Was the reading *good news* for the first audience? Why?

2. How might the reaction of the first audience suggest a direction for the homily?

3. Is the reading *good news* for you the preacher? Describe your response?

4. What experiences in the lives of your congregation suggest links to the reading?

- From news events
- From entertainment media (film, television, music, other arts)
- Conversations you have had with members of the congregation
- Particular issues of importance in your parish or local community

For Next Time

Prepare a brief summary of the significant issues you discovered in preparing one or more readings for your next homily. Just before playing the tape of your homily, explain to other group members how these insights influenced the way you prepared the homily.

5. Chapter Five: The Preacher's Own Faith

For Reflection and Discussion

These questions deal with a preacher's own faith. Group members may feel that certain questions and issues are private. If they choose not to discuss some issues in the group, they are asked to at least discuss how they would preach from those faith experiences.

1. Describe the person or event that most helps you see the face of God. How does this faith experience influence your homilies?

2. Preaching is the integration point of ministry. How do the following, or other aspects of your ministry, affect your preaching?

- Visits to hospital patients or the homebound
- Counseling or spiritual direction
- Personal study of the scriptures and theology
- Administrative duties
- Personal prayer
- Another experience not listed above

3. The chapter argues that preaching is a matter of a minister's identity, not just another function among many others. Discuss how some of the following experiences have made their way into a recent homily:

- A novel

- A film
- A conversation with a friend
- An encounter with some aspect of nature
- A news story
- Another experience not listed here

4. Preaching results when lived experience interacts with the faith of the church. Discuss the following questions and the way your answers might affect your homilies.

- What has God done for me lately?
- Why do I pray?
- What do I need from God?
- What happens in my life when I do not pray?
- Does God ever seem to ignore my prayer?
- What specifically has Jesus saved me *from*?
- What specifically has Jesus saved me *for*?
- Am I eager to experience eternal life? Would I like to begin today?
- Who are the people who most show me the face of God?

5. What has been your experience of Killinger's insight that preaching the scriptures forms the preacher?

> We are formed as we work at giving form to the Word of God. We become more and more like it as we study it and chisel at it and work it into our sermons; until at last, in rhythm with the Word that became flesh, our flesh in a very real sense becomes Word. [*The Centrality of Preaching in the Total Task of the Ministry*, (Waco, Tex.: Word, 1969), p. 35].

6. Without revealing the preacher's identity, give an example in which a homily has contained inappropriate self-disclosure. How might this preacher have presented the same message in an appropriate way?

7. Discuss the use of published homily services and/or complete homilies in light of the need to preach from your personal faith.

Activity

If group members have retained copies of former homilies, they can note how the face of God may have changed in their preaching over time. Write a brief "personality profile" of God as preached in a homily from several years ago. Compare it with a profile from a very recent homily. The following questions can serve as a guide. The group may also discuss these questions concerning the homily, "Come and See," from this chapter.

1. Is there one predominating image of God in the homily? (creator, redeemer, friend, angry judge, etc.)

2. At the time the homily was preached, was there a connection between this predominant image and any event occurring during your faith journey?

3. Does God expect anything from the congregation?

4. Does the face God described in the homily match the face of God in that liturgy's readings?

For Next Time

Use at least one instance of explicit faith witness in your next homily. Ask the group for feedback on the value of this witness.

6. Chapter Six: Listening to the Listeners

For Reflection and Discussion

Discuss each of the following assumptions about preaching as interaction between preachers and listeners described in Chapter Six. Refer to specific experience from your ministry.

- Preaching is the work of the Spirit within listeners as well as preachers.
- Preaching is an event of grace.
- Preaching names the grace already at work in the listeners.
- Preaching is about faith in Christ, not simply knowledge about Christ.
- Preaching often leads to surprising results.
- Preaching is the power to change, not the command that people should change.
- Preaching links the human story with God's story.

Activity

Do one of the following activities. Others may be done at later sessions.

1. Begin to prepare next Sunday's homily using the steps out-

lined in *Fulfilled in Your Hearing*.

2. Listen to a taped homily from a volunteer in the group. Evaluate the homily using the Feedback from the Pews in Chapter Six (pp. 136-137) designed for parish use.

3. Listen to a taped homily from a volunteer in the group. Evaluate a homily using the Homily Assessment Guidelines in Chapter Six (pp. 134-135).

For Next Time

Choose one of the assessment or feedback questionnaires for homily preparation or review described in this chapter (pp. 115-141).

7. Chapter Seven: Preaching the Prophetic Word

For Reflection and Discussion

1. Identify and discuss some sins or urgent social justice issues in your local community.

2. Pick an issue you discussed in the previous question. How would a moralist deal with this issue? How would you deal with this issue in a Sunday homily?

3. Discuss whether a specific issue of social justice could be preached no matter which readings are assigned to the liturgy.

4. Discuss each Guideline for Prophetic Preaching described in Chapter Seven.
- Preach God and nothing less.
- Preach for change.
- Preach as one who lives justice.
- Preach with compassion.
- Preach to the whole church.
- Preach to offer hope.

Activity

Analyze a homily on law and gospel.

1. Photocopy the sample homily at the end of Chapter Seven (pp. 156-160) for each group member. Working alone, use highlighters of two different colors to highlight occurrences of the law and of the gospel.

2. Compare your results. Discuss any discrepancies in your decisions about what constitutes law and what constitutes gospel.

3. If time remains, read next Sunday's gospel and/or the other readings for that Sunday. Discuss the social justice consequences you could preach in the homily.

For Next Time

1. Prepare next Sunday's homily with at least one specific reference to a social justice issue. Whatever the themes in the three readings, prepare the homily using the social justice issue as a consequence of Christian discipleship.

2. When your group meets to give feedback on one another's homilies, discuss the preacher's use of law and gospel. Was the preacher sensitive to moralizing?

8. Chapter Eight: Daily Homilies

For Reflection and Discussion

1. Describe the congregation that regularly attends a weekday Eucharist in your parish. You may wish to review the material from Chapter Six that describes exegeting the congregation.

2. How does your regular weekday congregation shape your preaching?

3. How might you adapt the sample weekday homily from Chapter Eight for your own congregation?

4. Discuss the sample homilies for funerals, weddings, and children in light of the suggested guidelines for that type of homily.

5. Discuss strategies that you have found helpful for preaching to children.

Activity

Choose one of these workshop activities. Each will require planning before the group meets.

1. Recall the details of the children's story, *Pinocchio*. What does it say to children about unconditional love and forgiveness as shown in the woodcarver father? How might this story help you preach to very small children?

2. Invite several parish directors of religious education to attend this session. Ask them to offer suggestions on preaching to children.

3. Ask your parishioners to comment briefly about what they find helpful in weekday homilies. What would they like to hear more about? Bring the tape to the session and listen to it and discuss their responses.

Bibliography

Abelly, Louis. *The Life of the Venerable Servant of God Vincent de Paul,* 3 vols. Ed. John Rybolt. New Rochelle, N.Y.: New City, 1993.

Allen, Ronald J. *Interpreting the Gospel: An Introduction to Preaching.* St. Louis: Chalice, 1998.

Anderson, George. "Preaching the Just Word: An Interview With Walter J. Burghardt." *America* 175.9 (1996): 10-14.

Aquinas Institute of Theology Faculty. *In the Company of Preachers.* Ed. Regina Siegfried and Edward Ruane. Collegeville, Minn.: Liturgical Press,1993.

Saint Augustine. *On Christian Doctrine.* Trans. D. W. Robertson, Jr. New York: Liberal Arts, 1958.

Barth, Karl. "The Need and Promise of Christian Preaching." In *The Word of God and The Word of Man.* Trans. Douglas Horton. New York: Harper, 1957, pp. 97-135.

The Bishops' Committee on Priestly Life and Ministry, National Conference of Catholic Bishops. *Fulfilled in Your Hearing: The Homily in the Sunday Assembly.* Washington, D.C.: United States Catholic Conference, 1982.

Bouchard, Charles. "Authentic Preaching on Moral Issues." In *In the Company of Preachers.* Ed. Regina Siegfried and Edward Ruane. Collegeville, Minn.: Liturgical Press,1993, pp. 191-209.

Brown, Raymond. "Preaching in the Acts of the Apostles." In *A New Look at Preaching.* Ed. John Burke. Wilmington, Del.: Michael Glazier, 1983, pp. 59-74.

Brueggemann, Walter. *The Prophetic Imagination.* Philadelphia: Fortress Press, 1978.

___. *Texts Under Negotiation: The Bible and Postmodern Imagination.* Minneapolis: Fortress Press, 1993.

Buechner, Frederick. "By Grace We Are Saved." *The Living Pulpit* 4.1 (1995): 5.

Burghardt, Walter J. Address. Aquinas Great Preacher of the Year Award. St. Louis, 28 April 1995.

___. "From Study to Proclamation." In *A New Look At Preaching.* Ed. John Burke. Wilmington, Del.: Michael Glazier, 1983, pp. 25-42.

___. *Preaching: The Art and the Craft.* New York: Paulist Press, 1987.

___. *Preaching the Just Word.* New Haven: Yale University Press, 1996.

Burke, John, ed. *A New Look at Preaching.* Wilmington, Del.: Michael Glazier, 1983.

Buttrick, David G. *Homiletic Moves and Structures*. Philadelphia: Fortress Press, 1987.

___. *Preaching the New and the Now*. Louisville: Westminster John Knox, 1998.

___. "Who Is Listening?" In *Listening to the Word: Studies in Honor of Fred B. Craddock*. Ed. Gail R. O'Day and Thomas G. Long. Nashville: Abingdon, 1993, pp. 189-206.

Cancro, Francis T. "To Live the Word with Little Folks." In *Preaching Better*. Ed. Frank J. McNulty. New York: Paulist Press, 1985, pp. 97-104.

Cannon, Kathleen. "Theology of the Word." In *The New Dictionary of Sacramental Worship*. Ed. Peter E. Fink. Collegeville, Minn.: Liturgical Press,1990, pp. 1323-31.

Catechism of the Catholic Church. (Second Edition) Washington, D.C.: United States Catholic Conference, 1997.

Code of Canon Law. Washington, D.C.: Canon Law Society of America, 1983.

Delaplane, Joan. "Spirituality of the Preacher." In *Concise Encyclopedia of Preaching*. Ed. William H. Willimon and Richard Lischer. Louisville: Westminster John Knox, 1995, pp. 448-50.

___. "The Living Word: An Overshadowing of the Spirit." In *In the Company of Preachers*. Ed. Regina Siegfried and Edward Ruane. Collegeville, Minn.: Liturgical Press,1993, pp. 141-50.

DeLeers, Stephen. "Written Text Becomes Living Word: Official Roman Catholic Teaching on the Homily, 1963-93." In *Papers of the Annual Meeting of the Academy of Homiletics* 1996, pp. 1-10.

Empereur, James L., and Christopher G. Kiesling. *The Liturgy That Does Justice*. Theology and Life Series 33. Collegeville, Minn.: Liturgical Press,1990.

Fischer, Edward. *Everybody Steals from God*. Notre Dame, Ind.: University of Notre Dame Press, 1977.

Fisher, Wallace E., *Who Dares to Preach?: The Challenge of Biblical Preaching*. Minneapolis: Augsburg, 1979.

Fitzmyer, Joseph A. "Historical Criticism: Its Role in Biblical Interpretation and Church Life." *Theological Studies* 50 (1989): 244-59.

___. *The Biblical Commission's Document* "The Interpretation of the Bible in the Church: Text and Commentary." Rome: Editrice Pontificio Instituto Biblico, 1995.

Flannery, Austin, gen. ed. Vatican Council II: *The Conciliar and Post*

Conciliar Documents. Northport, N.Y.: Costello, 1975.

Ghiselin, Brewster, ed. *The Creative Process.* New York: New American Library, 1952.

Greidanus, Sidney. *The Modern Preacher and the Ancient Text: Interpreting and Preaching Biblical Literature.* Grand Rapids: Eerdmans, 1988.

Heil, John Paul. *The Gospel of Mark As a Model for Action.* New York: Paulist Press, 1992.

Hilkert, Mary Catherine. *Naming Grace: Preaching and the Sacramental Imagination.* New York: Continuum, 1997.

International Commission on English in the Liturgy, trans. "Directory for Masses With Children," *The Roman Missal.* New York: Catholic Book Publishing Co., 1985, pp. 56-61.

___, trans. Order of *Christian Funerals.* Chicago: Liturgy Training Publications, 1989.

___, trans. "Rite of Marriage." In *The Rites of the Catholic Church.* New York: Pueblo, 1976.

Janowiak, Paul. *The Holy Preaching: The Sacramentality of the Word in the Liturgical Assembly.* Collegeville, Minn.: Liturgical Press, 2000.

John Paul II. *On Catechesis in Our Time* (Catechesi Tradendae). October 16, 1979.

Kane, Thomas A., ed. *Teaching Advanced Homiletics: Proceedings of the Weston Summer Institute.* Vol. 3. Newton, Mass.: Sophia, 1994.

Karris, Robert J. "The Gospel According the Luke." In *The New Jerome Biblical Commentary.* Ed. Raymond E. Brown, Joseph A. Fitzmyer, and Roland E. Murphy. Englwood Cliffs, N.J.: Prentice Hall, 1990, pp. 675-721.

Killinger, John. *The Centrality of Preaching in the Total Task of the Ministry.* Waco, Tex.: Word, 1969.

Lamott, Anne. *Bird by Bird: Some Instructions on Writing and Life.* New York: Pantheon, 1994.

Lechner, Robert. "Liturgical Preaching." *Worship* 37 (1962-63): 639-50.

Long, Thomas G. and Edward Farley, eds. *Preaching as a Theological Task: World, Gospel, Scripture.* Louisville: Westminster John Knox, 1996.

Lowry, Eugene L. *The Homiletical Plot: The Sermon as Narrative Art Form.* (Expanded Edition) Louisville: Westminster John Knox, 2001.

Malina, Bruce J. "Eyes-Heart." In *Biblical Social Values and Their Meanings: A Handbook*. Ed. John J. Pilch and Bruce J. Malina. Peabody, Mass.: Hendrickson, 1993, pp. 63-67.

___. "Reading Theory Perspective: Reading Luke-Acts." In *The Social World of Luke-Acts: Models for Interpretation*. Ed. Jerome H. Neyrey. Peabody, Mass.: Hendrickson, 1991, pp. 4-23.

Malina, Bruce J., and Jerome H. Neyrey. "First-Century Personality: Dyadic, Not Individual." In *The Social World of Luke-Acts: Models for Interpretation*. Ed., Jerome H. Neyrey. Peabody, Mass.: Henrickson, 1991, pp. 67-96.

___. "Honor and Shame in Luke-Acts: Pivotal Values of the Mediterranean World." In *The Social World of Luke-Acts: Models For Interpretation*, Ed. Jerome H. Neyrey. Peabody, Mass.: Henrickson, 1991, pp. 25-65.

Malina, Bruce J., and Richard L. Rohrbaugh. *Social-Science Commentary on the Synoptic Gospels*. Minneapolis: Fortress Press, 1992.

Maloney, Robert. Lent Letter to Members of the Congregation of the Mission, 1993.

McGeady, Mary Rose. *Are You Out There God?* USA: Covenant House, 1996.

McNamara, Robert F. *Catholic Sunday Preaching: The American Guidelines—1791-1975*. (Special Study Series) Washington, D.C.: Word of God Institute, 1975.

McNulty, Frank J., ed. *Preaching Better*. New York: Paulist Press, 1985.

Miller, Charles E. *Ordained to Preach: A Theology and Practice of Preaching*. New York: Alba House, 1992.

Mueser, Fred W. *Luther the Preacher*. Minneapolis: Augsburg, 1983.

___, and Stanley D. Schneider, eds. *Interpreting Luther's Legacy*. Minneapolis: Augsburg, 1969.

National Pastoral Life Center. "Called to be Catholic: Church in a Time of Peril." New York: National Pastoral Life Center, 1996.

Neyrey, Jerome H., ed. *The Social World of Luke-Acts: Models for Interpretation*. Peabody, Mass.: Hendrickson, 1991.

Nouwen, Henri J. *Creative Ministry*. Garden City, N.Y.: Doubleday, 1971.

Oakman, Douglas E. "Was Jesus a Peasant?: Implications for Reading the Samaritan Story [Luke 10:30-35]." *Biblical Theology Bulletin* 22 (1992): 126-34.

O'Malley, John W. *Praise and Blame in Renaissance Rome: Rhetoric,*

Doctrine and Reform in the Sacred Orators of the Papal Courts, c. 1450-1521. Durham, N.C.: Duke University Press, 1979.

Paul VI. *On Evangelization in the Modern World (Evangelii Nuntiandi)*. Dec. 8, 1975.

___. Address to the Members of the *Consilium de Laicis* (October 2, 1974) *Acta Apostolicae Sedis* 66. (1974).

Pazdan, Mary Margaret. "Hermeneutics and Proclaiming the Sunday Readings." In *In the Company of Preachers*. Ed. Regina Siegfried and Edward Ruane. Collegeville, Minn.: Liturgical Press,1993, pp. 26-37.

Pilch, John J., and Bruce J. Malina, eds. *Biblical Social Values and Their Meanings: A Handbook*. Peabody, Mass.: Hendrickson, 1993.

Pilla, Anthony. "Ministry of the Word." *Origins* 25 (1995): 277-87.

Plevnik, Joseph. "Honor/Shame." In *Biblical Social Values and Their Meanings: A Handbook*. Ed. John J. Pilch and Bruce J. Malina. Peabody, Mass.: Hendrickson, 1993, pp. 95-104.

Pontifical Biblical Commission. "The Interpretation of the Bible in the Church." *Origins* 23 (1994): 498-524.

Rahner, Karl. "Priest and Poet." *Theological Investigations*. Vol. III. Trans. Karl H. and Boniface Kruger. Baltimore: Helicon Press, 1967, pp. 294-317.

___. "The Word and the Eucharist." *Theological Investigations*. Vol. IV. Trans. Kevin Smyth. Baltimore: Helicon Press, 1966, pp. 256-86.

Reid, Barbara E. *Parables for Preachers: The Gospel of Mark*. Collegeville, Minn.: Liturgical Press, 1999.

Richard, William A. "The Funeral Homily: Personal, But Not a Eulogy." *Church* (Summer 1992): 17-21.

Ricoeur, Paul. *Figuring the Sacred*. Trans. David Pellauer. Ed. Mark I. Wallace. Minneapolis: Fortress Press, 1995.

Ruane, Edward. "The Spirituality of a Preacher." In *In the Company of Preachers*. Ed. Regina Siegfried and Edward Ruane. Collegeville, Minn.: Liturgical Press,1993, pp. 151-64.

Rueter, Alvin. *Making Good Preaching Better: A Step-by-Step Guide to Scripture-Based, People-Centered Preaching*. Collegeville, Minn.: Liturgical Press,1997.

Saliers, Don. "Prayer." In *Concise Encyclopedia of Preaching*. Ed. William H. Willimon and Richard Lischer. Louisville: Westminster John Knox, 1995, pp. 377-78.

Schlafer, David. J. *Surviving the Sermon: A Guide to Preaching for Those Who Have to Listen*. Cambridge, Mass.: Cowley, 1992.

Shea, John. *Stories of God [An Unauthorized Biography]*. Allen, Tex.: Thomas More, 1978.

Smith, Christine M., ed. *Preaching Justice: Ethnic and Cultural Perspectives*. Cleveland: United Church, 1998.

Synod of Bishops. "Justice in the World." November 30, 1971. *Official Catholic Teachings: Social Justice*. Ed. Vincent P. Mainelli. Wilmington, Del.: McGrath, 1978, pp. 284-302.

Tappert, Theodore G., ed. *The Book of Concord: The Confessions of the Evangelical Lutheran Church*. Philadelphia: Muhlenberg, 1959.

Thompson, Clarence. "The Right Brain Language of Power." In *Preaching Better*. Ed. Frank J. McNulty. Mahwah, N.J.: Paulist Press, 1985, pp. 87-94.

Tisdale, Leona Tubbs. "Congregation." In *Concise Encyclopedia of Preaching*. Ed. William H. Willimon and Richard Lischer. Louisville: Westminster/Knox, 1995, pp. 87-89.

Troeger, Thomas. *Ten Strategies for Preaching in a Multi-Media Culture*. Nashville: Abingdon, 1996.

Van Harn, Roger E. *Pew Rights: For People Who Listen to Sermons*. Grand Rapids: Eerdmans, 1992.

Van Linden, Philip. *The Gospel of Luke and Acts*. Wilmington, Del.: Michael Glazier, 1986.

Vawter, Bruce, "Introduction to Prophetic Literature." In *The New Jerome Biblical Commentary*. Ed. Raymond E. Brown, Joseph A. Fitzmyer, and Roland E. Murphy. Englewood Cliffs, N.J.: Prentice Hall, 1990, 1968, pp. 186-200.

Viviano, Benedict T., "The Gospel According to Matthew." In *The New Jerome Biblical Commentary*, Ed. Raymond E. Brown, Joseph A. Fitzmyer, and Roland E. Murphy. Englewood Cliffs, N.J.: Prentice Hall, 1990, 1968, pp. 630-74.

Walther, C. God's No and God's Yes: *The Proper Distinction Between Law and Gospel*. Cond., Walter C. Pieper. St. Louis: Concordia, 1973.

Wardlaw, Don M., ed. *Learning Preaching: Understanding & Participating in the Process*. Lincoln, Ill.: Lincoln Christian, 1989.

Waznak, Robert. "The Catechism and The Sunday Homily." *America* 22 October 1994: 18-21.

___. "Homily." In *The New Dictionary of Sacramental Worship*. Ed.

Peter E. Fink. Collegeville, Minn.: Liturgical Press,1990, pp. 552-58.

___. *An Introduction to the Homily*. Collegeville, Minn.: Liturgical Press, 1999.

Webb, Joseph M. *Preaching and the Challenge of Pluralism*. St. Louis, Chalice, 1998.

___. *Old Texts, New Sermons: The Quiet Revolution in Biblical Preaching*. St. Louis: Chalice, 2000.

Willimon, William H., and Richard Lischer, eds. *Concise Encyclopedia of Preaching*. Louisville: Westminster John Knox, 1995.

Wilson, P. S. *A Concise History of Preaching*. Nashville: Abingdon, 1992.

___. "Imagination." In *Concise Encyclopedia of Preaching*. Ed. William H. Willimon and Richard Lischer. Louisville: Westminster John Knox, 1995, pp. 266-69.

Additional Professional Resources

THE ART OF THEOLOGICAL REFLECTION
Connecting Faith and Life
JOHN SHEA
A clear, practical explanation of how to see the religious implications and presence of God in everyday life. The six audio tapes are filled with the clear explanations and vivid examples that are the hallmark of this noted theologian and storyteller.
Six 60- to 90-minute audio cassettes, $29.95

MEDITATIONS FOR MINISTERS
MARK G. BOYER
Over 300 brief reflections address theological, spiritual and sacramental topics, themes and concerns along with pastoral, professional and personal issues of faith and life. Each brief meditation concludes with a Bible verse.
160 pages, paperback, $9.95

SPIRITUALITY AND HEALTH CARE
Reaching Toward a Holistic Future
JOHN SHEA
A thoughtful consideration of the current dialogue between health care and ministry professionals on the role of spirituality in a holistic approach to health care. A unique look at the spiritual interests of patients, caregivers, chaplains and healthcare organizations.
144 pages, paperback, $12.95

A CONTEMPORARY CELTIC PRAYER BOOK
WILLIAM JOHN FITZGERALD
Foreword by JOYCE RUPP
A beautiful prayer book that captures the flavor and sensibility of traditional Celtic spirituality for today's busy people. The first part of the book contains a simplified Liturgy of the Hours. The second part is a treasury of Celtic prayers, blessings and rituals.
160 pages, paperback, $9.95

Available from booksellers
or call 800-397-2282 in the US and Canada